The New Leaders of Change

'*The New Leaders of Change* gives us an intimate view of how the new generation of leaders are defining leadership, change, and transformation. Their mandate is clear: regardless of the type of business you're in, the B-to-B world, the B-to-C world, the C-to-C world, or the A-to-Z world, business is fundamentally H-to-H, human to human. Maitri O'Brien documents that the value of empathy, compassion, courage, and collaboration are more relevant today and they are making a comeback. In the process, O'Brien liberates the term "humanity" from the stigma of being "too subjective", and not "true science", and inspires us to embrace our humanity as a path to building a sustainable and forward-thinking workplace that thrives during times of exponential change.'

Chip Conley
Founder, Modern Elder Academy

'Nobody should *just* read this book. All you must do is to deeply digest every single sentence, one after the other, and reflect on them for the rest of your day. This book is a lifetime journey. Stunning.'

Beat Geissler
Activist-Entrepreneur, Family Man and Biker
Berlin, Palo Alto, Zurich

'We live in a VUCA world: volatile, uncertain, complex and ambiguous. This requires the next generation of leaders to rethink how they make decisions, plan forward, manage risk and foster change. *The New Leaders of Change* provides an in-depth view of how brilliant young leaders take on this challenge – with passion and by taking their heart to work.'

Professor Dr Uwe Krueger
Head Europe, Middle East & Africa
Temasek International, Singapore

'*The New Leaders of Change* is an insightful and very timely book for leaders of all ages who want to lead with purpose, for people and the planet. The new generation of leaders in the book convince us it is time to shift from the bureaucratic, top-down, command and control ways of leading, and bring humanity back into the workplace. As leaders, we have a responsibility to care for people – employees, customers, partners – as well as the communities we work in, and the planet we inhabit. I found myself cheering throughout the book and thinking, yes, this is the new paradigm of leadership we need.'

Armin Meier
Owner, Boyden, Switzerland
Chairman and member of non-executive boards

'With an authoritative, engaging and pragmatic style, *The New Leaders of Change* explores how we listen and understand the new generation of leaders, how we learn from them, and how to evolve with them to bring about effective and much-needed change. Specifically, how we use a people-centered lens in an innovative, fresh way and how we harness their passion for purpose, meaning, diversity and inclusion and saving the planet. Developed from thoughtful research and a diverse set of interviews, *The New Leaders of Change* not only provides rich and useful insights but is told against a backdrop of an incredibly engaging personal story; proof of Maitri's life-long experience of dealing with change, and her passion for guiding the next generation of leaders. *The New Leaders of Change* is a great resource for anyone who wants to drive successful change today and, more importantly, who wants to understand how to successfully support and pass the baton onto our next generation of leaders.'

Karen Gaydon
Chief People Officer, Board Member and Operating Partner

MAITRI O'BRIEN

The NEW LEADERS *of* CHANGE

How Next Generation Leaders
are Transforming Themselves,
their Businesses and the World
with Purpose and Empathy

PCL

First published 2022 by PCL Publishing,
100 Church Street, Brighton, BN1 1UJ, United Kingdom

ISBN 978-1-905587-11-7 (hardback)

ISBN 978-1-905587-13-1 (paperback)

A catalogue record for this book is available
from the British Library in the UK

COVER ART

The artwork on the cover is inspired by Mira O'Brien's work

BULK COPIES

To order multiple copies of *The New Leaders of Change* for a workshop or event you're running contact Maitri O'Brien at maitriobrien.com

DEDICATION

To the New Leaders of Change, you are the heart and soul of this book. Being purpose driven is a catalyst for change. This book documents how much real change is driven by you, the New Leaders of Change. I am awestruck by your humanity, curiosity, compassion, and courage – and I am committed to amplifying and enabling your leadership to shine.

To my grandparents and parents whose vision, courage, and resilience made all things possible.

To my husband for trusting my vision, for supporting, encouraging, and tolerating me for two years as I obsessed about this book.

And with infinite love and affection, to my grand-daughter Frida Magnolia O'Brien.

CONTENTS

PART III: CHANGE

THE HUMAN EXPERIENCE REVOLUTION

TABLES AND FIGURES

APPENDICES

Foreword

JOHANNES RECK

CO-FOUNDER & CEO, GET YOUR GUIDE

If you take away anything from this book, remember this: we are embarking on defining a new leadership paradigm for the new generation of leaders. It is a people-centered paradigm that places human experience at the core of everything.

Now that I have your attention, let me explain.

Welcome to the human experience revolution, the most fantastic time to be alive. We are living in the middle of exponential technological change and the beginnings of the human experience revolution. The internet connects us all, and taps into collective intelligence and talents worldwide. Never before have we had this much power and opportunity to change the world on a grand scale. These technologies force us to be more deliberate and thoughtful about how to better understand and enhance the human experience. We need to be sure that these technologies elevate and enrich the human experience and, more importantly, do not diminish it.

As the next generation of leaders, we need to ask, 'What kinds of experiences are most rewarding and enriching? What are the characteristics of meaningful experiences? How do we create experiences that offer happiness, belonging, and connectedness?'

These are the questions my team and I at Get Your Guide think about every day as we work toward our mission to provide unforgettable experiences for all sectors of society on a global scale. Our customers, partners, colleagues, communities, and investors are all human beings motivated by the possibility of connecting through experiences.

For me, the future of business is about having the courage to embrace our humanity with each other. It is a revolution that demands a new vision obsessively focused on human experience and relationships. It requires businesses to organize around people (customers, employees, partners, communities) and purpose versus only profit. I believe it is the next critical business imperative to weather disruption and uncertainty, engage all key stakeholders, and achieve the differentiation required for growth.

'We need a new leadership playbook'

Maitri O'Brien's book *The New Leaders of Change* shows that we are forging new approaches to business, leadership, and citizenship. And it's commendable because we need a new leadership playbook, grounded in authentic connection, purpose, transparency, and trust. We need a new paradigm where the leaders of tomorrow challenge the long-held beliefs of why companies exist. Do we have a compelling company story that inspires employees, excites partners, attracts customers, and engages communities? How are we designing our organizations, processes, products, and culture based on human experience design?

If the Covid-19 pandemic showed us anything, it's that people are not anonymous parts of a business. People are the business – its most important and powerful asset. When the Covid-19 lockdown halted our company, our revenue was zero, and we were in grave crisis. The tourism industry was destroyed, and the idea of selling 'experiences' was an unreality, given border closures, and the closing of attractions and museums. As the pandemic continued into 2021, we realized the real crisis was the impact on our employees' morale, wellbeing, and motivation. How could we continue to engage our people in a business during the pandemic? How could we continually engage and help our partners, many of them small business owners? My biggest fears and concerns centered around people, less so on our business's strategic, financial, or technical aspects.

We found some innovative ways to motivate employees by offering a generous salary-for-equity program. And 98 per cent of our eligible workforce participated in the program and accepted a 30 per cent salary cut on average. Although we unfortunately had to lay off some employees, our attrition rate was very low. I was really humbled by the commitment and loyalty of our employees to Get Your Guide's mission, leadership, and future.

The second area we focused on was improving our product, both on the tech and inventory sides, working with our partners. Obviously, they were struggling for business and were thrilled to work with us to help improve our products. In addition, they were motivated to negotiate new deals with us and help accelerate our recovery. Now, coming out of Covid-19, travel is bouncing back and we are well above 2019 levels.

A key factor in this was the decision to put people at the center, to keep them productive, energized, and engaged to restore their confidence.

The continuing challenge, then, for leaders and society is to navigate the changes introduced by technological innovation – changes such as Artificial Intelligence and the metaverse – and to define the next frontier of human experience. Because we have a shared need for rich and emotional experiences – we need belonging, connection, and empathy. Yet while technology has enabled us to connect, communicate, and collaborate in extraordinary ways, it also has the potential to leave us less human and more isolated. If we live more through screens in virtual worlds, however, we limit our human experience to a narrow, controlled, and abstract world. Paradoxically, in our tech-driven world, innovation, growth, and agility largely depend on people. This is why I'm super critical of the idea that we'll all be living in a matrix in a couple of years.

Here's an example, close to my heart. During the Covid-19 lockdown we launched a travel-from-home series on YouTube hosted by some of our suppliers. People briefly latched on to it, but it did not capture nearly the same experience for them as it would in person. Because people want to interact with each other in person. The internet can never replace real-life experiences.

When exploring a new city, our customers want to interact with tour guides in person. A great tour guide connects them with the local community. They learn new ways of seeing, thinking, and doing. And perhaps they question whether 'the way things are' in their own context is the only way to be. This is something I'm very interested in: how do we continue to connect people across the globe and unlock transformative experiences? I believe this is the way we can facilitate global change.

In a very real sense I am a technologist, but I am also an optimist about the future of technology and the digital world. Yes, we will continue to see exponential changes in business, economy, and society, but I believe those changes will be for the better, even though there are some dark possibilities. Putting those possibilities aside, though, I see technology as an enabler. It enables accountability, social trust, and transparency. And importantly I believe the virtual experiences that are emerging do not end the human experience; they are transforming it into something new. And as long as we are diligent, engaged, and proactive in defining the role of technology, we can use it to elevate the human experience.

I am optimistic because I feel a sense of personal responsibility and agency for being part of that change. Reading *The New Leaders of Change* increases my optimism because my generation of leaders are hopeful and want to be part of that change.

My personal mission is to unlock incredible travel experiences for our Get Your Guide customers. But beyond that, I want to unlock as much talent and human potential around me as possible.

I am a big supporter of the new generation of entrepreneurs and leaders. I support them through funding, introducing them to my network, and personal mentoring. I am genuinely curious about who they are as people, their passion, and how they can innovate for their customers and impact the world. I invest a lot of time enabling young entrepreneurs and passing on the knowledge that I've been fortunate to learn over the last 10 years.

And in *The New Leaders of Change*, Maitri O'Brien offers an intimate look at what this new world led by the new generation of leaders will look like – and how change must happen at multiple levels: personal, interpersonal, organizational, and in the world as a whole. She shows us that people are at the heart of the business. Our shared humanity is actively expressed, she shows, through compassion, curiosity, collaboration, and connectedness with other people.

It is an impressive effort to collect the stories of a new generation of leaders who have set out to change the world and to forge their own paths for growth and success. It inspires me to consider how I can be a better person and put people in the center of my leadership every day and with every interaction. Maitri O'Brien holds up a mirror to remind us what is possible when we embrace and develop our own humanity and see all the opportunity, potential, and power we are not leveraging.

In summary, Maitri O'Brien has captured the *zeitgeist* of the new generation of leadership, living at the intersection of technology, people, environment, communities, and business. She nails the distinctly unique new generational traits:

- We are the first generation of digital natives. We came of age as the internet was coming of age. Anyone can tell the story of themselves, in words, pictures, and videos, to an audience of one or 10 or 100 or (if their content goes viral) a million or more. This level of global connection and personal access through technology makes our generation unique and unified.

- We believe in the collective intelligence, power, and wisdom of teams and communities. We know a small group or community of purpose-driven people can accomplish change that was once only possible by governments and large corporations. We created the thousands of 'shared economy' enterprises that rely on our willingness to trust and engage with one another.

- We value activities – at work and personally – that are purposeful and meaningful. We value helping others and working to improve communities and the world. We demonstrate empathy, compassion, and courage.

- We challenge tired concepts such as hierarchy, top-down control, authority, and preserving the *status quo*. Instead, we prefer collaboration, listening to diverse views, and harnessing the power of the collective.

- We are the catalyst for business, politics, and technology change. We are the innovators of the future. We are revolutionizing industries and possess the courage to stay committed to our mission in the face of adversity.

- We are curious and have a passion for learning and exploring new experiences. Numerous studies have found that our generation would rather spend money on 'experiences' than purchasing material goods.

In this pivotal moment where digital and physical become more integrated, the leaders of tomorrow seem to understand the fundamentals of designing human experience – what makes people motivated, inspired, ambitious, and committed. Although yesterday's leadership depended on a single heroic leader's vision and ambition, we believe meaningful experience design emerges from collaboration with customers, employees, and partners to create a compelling story collectively.

The new leadership paradigm in *The New Leaders of Change* offers a clear alternative to the traditional command-and-control leadership models of the last century. Maitri O'Brien points us toward creating more positive human experiences through adopting people-centric leadership. And creating a workplace environment built on creativity, collaboration, and agility, where employees do meaningful work and connect their personal purpose to the company's purpose.

The New Leaders of Change is not a story about cynicism and 'checking out' – which so many other writers have wrongly surmised – it is an optimistic story. What sets this book apart is that it is about the new generation of leaders 'taking the leap' at one of the most pivotal moments in human history. We have the opportunity to have an exponential impact for people all over the world.

So we have to allow ourselves to dream big to solve the challenges we face worldwide. This is a hands-on-deck moment. We are in the right place and time to lead change. We can define what it means to be successful in our generation and create our legacy – doing work that contributes to making things better for people, communities, and the planet. We have the opportunity to step up to our greatness and be not just the next generation, but the greatest generation that ever lived.

What Maitri O'Brien has observed from the front lines – and what you will come to understand as you read this book – is that no businesses, governments, or public institutions can keep up with the pace of change set by technological innovations. To do so requires something radically new – a vision of leadership and organizations that leverage technology and innovation at speed and scale while putting people at the center.

For this reason, I can't think of a more perfect guide for those CEOs and executives interested in thriving during this time of disruptive change. The stories of leaders in this book will inspire the next generation of leaders to act on their passion in life, and help older generations learn how the new generation of leaders approach leadership, change, and transformation.

In conclusion, I say this: anyone who is part of the new generation of leaders, and all aspiring changemakers, should read this book.

Johannes Reck
Berlin, Germany

Author's Preface

THE NEW LEADERS OF CHANGE

Change is continuous, ubiquitous, and exponential. It is the natural evolution of business. And it is omnipresent. No matter the day, the hour, or the moment, change is with us in every aspect of our lives.

Change, however, is not something that can be managed through a step-wise process with a start point and an end point. Linear thinking can never catch up with the changing world we see around us every day. Our changing world is simply too fast, too unpredictable and, frankly, too complex for that.

Given this scenario, it should be blindingly obvious that the world needs a new form of leadership – one that is better equipped to navigate unprecedented levels of change. Sad to say, not everyone sees this. Yet.

So in this book I want to show you why we need leaders who can inspire and lead people towards a unifying vision, but leaders who at the same time are catalysts for constant change. It sounds like a paradox, but I assure you it isn't.

We also need leaders who can make tough decisions, take bold actions and take dramatic risks. Because who knows where the change facing us will lead. If change is one thing, it is certainly unpredictable.

So it's going to require a shared purpose as we embark on this, and agility to navigate the terrain – from all of us in the game. It's also going to require an almost unlimited supply of empathy. Because we need to keep all of our key stakeholders front and center – at all costs. And that itself requires bold action on our part. So where do we start if we at least want to hang on to the coat-tails of change?

Well, every change we seek to steer, every innovation we want to introduce, starts with a human-to-human connection. So above all, the change catalysts of the future need to demonstrate the key humanistic values of authenticity, empathy, compassion, and trust. We need to put people at the heart of change.

Secondly, in a world where change is continuous, ubiquitous, and exponential, leaders will need to evolve continuously themselves. How can you keep up with constantly evolving change unless you yourself, your team, and your organization constantly evolve too?

But what does that involve? Well, we must continually learn and re-learn what it means to be people-centered. We must constantly relearn how technology can help us, as it too changes dramatically. And we must let go of the old mental maps and the old assumptions that got us here in the first place. Because, let's face it, transformational change is messy.

Luckily some people do get the message. Some people are having tremendous success experimenting, iterating, and above all being people-centered in their lives and in the workplace. I call these people the New Leaders of Change. And I've named this book after them.

Let me share their stories with you now – because they will inspire you to look again at yourself, at your leadership future, and at what you can bring to the people around you.

WHAT YOU'LL GET OUT OF THIS BOOK

The New Leaders of Change is the result of my lifetime of experience leading change – from Silicon Valley to the Far East and now at the heart of Europe – and it showcases the headline results from almost two years of solid research. At the heart of the book are my in-depth interviews with more than 50 executives – from around the world, and from organizations of every size. But don't worry. Although it's been a massive data-gathering project, I've concentrated mainly on the stories I've been told. I wanted to create what I hope is a very readable book. After all, it's the stories and emotions of my interviewees that carry their convictions and lessons the best.

In practical terms, the book is divided into three sections. First, I'll share the new context of change facing you as a leader, and also explode the long-standing myth that you can manage change. That's in Chapter 1. Then, in Chapters 2-5, we'll look at the distinctive attributes that the New Leaders of Change demonstrate so clearly. From agility to innovation, from having immense empathy to helping firms define an over-arching sense of purpose.

And in the third part we'll look at how the New Leaders of Change at the heart of this book handle change at the individual, team, and organizational levels. Because – make no mistake – they demonstrate path-finding ways to make a real difference at every level.

Finally, in Chapter 10 I'll pull together all the strands from the research and share two models of people-centered change to help you reflect on the characteristics you need to enhance your own skills and impact as a leader.

ACKNOWLEDGEMENTS

The Web of Collaboration

I express my profound gratitude to the many co-creators of this labor of love.

It has been a privilege to work with Jacqueline Moore and Steven Sonsino, they are my editors; however, they have been much more! Their enthusiasm and belief in this project has at times exceeded even my own. I am grateful to Jacqueline and Steven for gently directing, coaching, firmly nudging and shepherding this book and this author along. On every level they have enhanced these pages and my experience of being a first-time author. I would be lost without them.

I express my profound gratitude to those invisible collaborators – family, friends, colleagues, clients, and teachers. They have shaped my worldview, my thinking, and my sense of self – as a daughter, wife, mother, friend, professional woman, and lifelong student. And to all the authors who have shaped me intellectually and inspired me to write this book.

I am truly blessed to have a daughter who is an artist. Watching her master her craft over the years, I realized that business leaders can learn a lot from the artist's path. Artists are continually experimenting, interpreting, testing different methods and having the courage to make their work public. The artwork on the book cover as well as on the book website are inspired by Mira O'Brien's work.

STAY CONNECTED

If you want to develop your thinking and your skills further as a leader of change then in the appendices I share a bibliography and some notes. They're in the appendices because I want to keep the main body of the book as readable as possible. There are also some additional resources you might like to take a look at. They'll be valuable if you're serious about further self-development, or if you're looking for some help to apply the new tools within your own organization.

If you want to get in touch with me personally – to tell me what you make of the research, or to share your stories and insights for the next volume – you can reach me on LinkedIn or at my website. I look forward to hearing from you soon.

Maitri O'Brien
Zurich, Switzerland
maitriobrien.com

CAST OF CHARACTERS

Anne-Sophie d'Andlau (FRANCE)
Co-founder and Managing Partner at CIAM

Nico Arcino (USA)
Head of Strategic Partnerships at Kaiser Permanente

Martin Baart (GERMANY)
Co-founder and CEO at Ecoligo

Stephen Baines (UK)
Lead Solutions Consultant, Salesforce

Banks Baker (USA)
Head of Global Partnerships (Search Content) at Google

Venetia Bell (UK)
Group Chief Sustainability Officer
and Head of Strategy at GIB Asset Management

Leah Belsky (USA)
Chief Enterprise Officer at Coursera

Kim Bertz (USA)
Senior Vice President, Workplace Services & Experience at Wells Fargo

Andrea Buetler (SINGAPORE)
Director of Energy Transition Sales, Asia Pacific, at Worley

Trevor Campbell (JAPAN)
VP Sales – APAC, at Tapjoy

Nirupa Chander (SINGAPORE)
Managing Director, Singapore, at Hitachi Energy

Chip Conley (USA)
Founder, Modern Elder Academy, hotelier, hospitality entrepreneur, author and speaker

Lindsey Crawford (USA)
Brand Strategy and Creative Consultant at Thermos

Linda Dörig (SWITZERLAND)
Head of Supplier Development at Gebana

Fonta Hadley (USA)
Owner and Founder of Eloquence

Jan Hase (GERMANY)
Co-founder and CEO at Wunderflats

Tara Hovey (USA)
President and Chief Executive Officer at Optima

Katy Hutchinson (IRELAND)
Senior Equity Research Analyst, Impax Asset Management

Tristan Jackson (USA)
Chief Strategy Officer and Co-founder of VECKTA

Kevin Jolly (GERMANY)
Head of Business Analytics at TIER Mobility

Arpit Kaushik (UK)
CEO at Hypha

Thomas Klein (GERMANY)
People and Organization Leader at Jodel

Katie Koch (USA)
Co-head, Fundamental Equity Business, at Goldman Sachs Asset Management

Christy Lake (USA)
Chief People Officer at Twilio Inc

Catherine Li (HONG KONG SAR)
CEO, Asia Pacific, at Atkins

Rubin Lind (GERMANY)
CEO and Founder, Skills4School

Adrian Locher (GERMANY)
CEO and Founder, Merantix Venture Studio

Johnny Luk (UK)
Senior Associate at Global Counsel

Jonas Muff (GERMANY)
CEO and Founder, Vara. Former CEO, MX Healthcare

Aman Narain (SINGAPORE)
Global New Payments Ecosystems Lead at Google

Jayson Noland (USA)
Head of Investor Relations at Cloudflare

Nikita Nosov (USA)
Global Operations Director at Flexport

Debbie O'Neill (USA)
VP – Domestic Partnerships, at Honey, acquired by Paypal

Paulo Pontin (BRAZIL)
Managing Partner – Latin America, at Verizon Enterprise Solutions

Adnan Raza (USA)
CFO at PDF Solutions

Andrea Ruotolo (CANADA)
Senior Director, Grid Modernization and Innovation, at Liberty Utilities

Donna See (SINGAPORE)
CEO at Xora Innovation

Erika Velazquez (SWITZERLAND)
AVP Digital Ecosystem Manager, Electrification Business at ABB

Felicia Würtenberger (GERMANY)
Humans, Vibes and Structure (CHRO) at Flooz

Also many thanks to the following for their invaluable contributions to this book: *Jennifer Adams, Britta Bibel-Cavallaro, Rimma Boshernitsan, João Paulo Figueira, Kevin Meisel, Bettina Nebermann, Niclas Nowotny, Angad Pal, Alexander Sprey, and Alicia Stevenson.*

The NEW LEADERS of CHANGE

PART 1: CONTEXT

LEADING EXPONENTIAL CHANGE

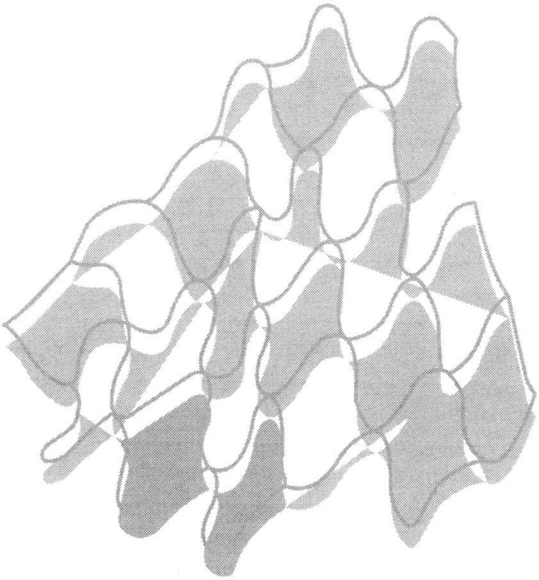

Introduction
A PERSONAL STORY

Why do I do what I do? What made me decide to make a career in change and transformation? I have often been asked these questions by the leaders I interviewed during my research for this book. First it was how have I managed to craft such a career when it wasn't possible to get a degree in change and transformation? And now it's what has inspired me to write a book on change, transformation, and the new generation of leaders?

The fact that I chose to devote my professional life to change and transformation is not an accident; it was my inheritance. I come from three generations of refugees and immigrants. My grandparents on both sides are from Uzbekistan and had to flee their home suddenly to escape death at the hands of the Soviet Union's army. They literally walked over the mountains to Afghanistan and lived in refugee camps. Imagine the level of disruption, uncertainty, and displacement they experienced.

From all the stories I have been told, a few images have stayed with me. One is a picture of a teenage girl and her young mother saying goodbye on a dock as people hurry to get on board a ship. The teenage girl is confused and her mother is grief-stricken but determined to ensure she gets on that ship.

The teenage girl was my mother. My mother's life, my own, my daughter's, and granddaughter's lives have been possible because my grandmother made the heart-wrenching decision to smuggle my mother, aged 14, on to a ship bound for a country she knew nothing about.

She relied on a neighbor to keep her safe until she could find a way to reunite with her daughter.

At that time my grandmother was a young widow with three other children living in Afghanistan's refugee camps. Eventually she married an Afghan who had been threatening to sell my mother as a child bride to a well-established landlord. My mother and her caretakers were bound for Turkey where they could make a new start as Turkish citizens, a coveted status for people who had given up their homes, wealth, families, and dignity to escape the atrocities of the Soviet Union when it took over Uzbekistan. It would be several years before my grandmother and three uncles were reunited with my mother.

I have been told that story throughout my life; however, it was only recently that I really understood its power. A single decision by my grandmother has produced such an enormous ripple effect for three generations.

Another picture that has stayed with me is of a 12-year-old small and awkward girl dressed in her finest clothes, waiting to board a 747 Lufthansa plane to New York. She had been left behind with her grandmothers and her extended family while her mother, father, and two younger brothers tried to weave together a life in the United States. She and her older sister were left behind because the family didn't have enough money to buy tickets for all four kids, so they had taken only the two young boys.

The young girl all alone was myself. I remember packing my small suitcase to join my family, flying all the way from Istanbul to New York on my own although I had never been in an airplane before. I was full of fear, excitement, and questions. After two years of separation, would my brothers like me? What would it be like to live in New York? Were my parents rich Americans like I'd seen in a movie? How would I ever learn the language?

Narratives of displaced people – the stories of my grandparents and parents and myself – often invoke sensations of trauma, of separation and dislocation, and this is certainly a significant aspect of their experience. But such narratives are also full of optimism, courage, growth, adaptability, resilience, and new beginnings. Having the courage and audacity to imagine a better world, if not for yourself then for your children and grandchildren.

The scale of change and disruption to the lives of three generations of my family was huge and complicated. Our lives were constantly pulled apart and put together within a completely new context – a new country, culture, and language. However, I believe disruption and change can be a positive force and a gateway to new and rich opportunities that enrich your life.

Now, if this were a movie version of my life, I would land in New York as a young girl, learn to speak English, excel in school, attend a respectable university, and attain the American dream of the good life. I would continually remember the sacrifices my grandmother and my mother made, and I would know exactly what I needed to do to live up to my potential and have the courage to follow my dreams. But my life is not a movie. I am not a character. I don't have a script, producer or director. And sometimes – perhaps even most of the time – life is messy with many disruptions, opportunities, and forks in the road

As I learned to speak English more fluently and entered my teenage years, I embedded myself in 1970s US teenage culture. I refused to speak Turkish or acknowledge my Uzbek roots. It seemed like a distant fable to me.

I went on to university, becoming a normal American university student and participating in everything my peers thought was cool. I was taking a pharmacology degree. Why pharmacology? Well, my parents thought it was a respectable profession and would ensure I have a good job at the local pharmacy. Just like it was prescribed that my sister would be an engineer and my brothers would be teachers.

The next transformative change in my life came when I was in my third year. It was a time when I felt lost and fragmented as I negotiated multiple cultures and expectations. Just when I thought I could no longer solve one more organic chemistry problem, I was introduced to meditation by my marketing professor. To ignite our creativity and inspiration, he had us listen to some ancient-sounding chants and meditate.

Soon after, I found myself on a plane to India to study with my professor's meditation teacher. It was heartbreaking to tell my parents I found no joy in pharmacology and was going to India to live in an ashram and study yoga and meditation. Central to the guru's teachings were the directions to 'See God in each other' and 'Honor yourself. Meditate to get in touch with your true self. God dwells within you as you.'

When I heard the teachings of the guru, it made sense to me. I had to travel 8,000 miles back to the East, to India, to find myself and put the puzzle pieces back together.

I am not sure if I ever found God inside myself; however, I learned some life-long tools such as meditation, reflection, and equanimity – a mental attitude of balance, non-judgment, and the ability to manage situations of stress, change, and disruption.

My next evolution was to apply myself to the hard work of cultivating my own talent, my purpose, and my life's work – which has been a continuous journey really, not a destination. And for me, that has meant many things. Such as being a mother. Such as studying psychology for individuals and organizations. Such as investing 25+ years in a career focused on change, transformation, and leadership. Such as working globally with a diverse set of countries, cultures, and companies. And now, it is writing this book. And for me, that intersection of change, courage, and resilience feels like my mission and my superpower.

I wrote this book between the spring of 2020 and the fall of 2021 – a period during which everything changed. In evolutionary science, there's a theory about the way species evolve. It's called punctuated equilibrium: long periods of stability where not much changes, followed by significant amounts of evolutionary change in short, stressful bursts of time. Evolutionary change is not a constant, iterative, and gradual process – it occurs in environments of disruption, crisis, and volatility. We are going through such a period right now.

The Covid-19 pandemic shattered our illusion of immortality and individuality. We have had a collective, shared experience of various states of lockdown, with schools and offices closed, masks on, and all our interactions with the external world taking place via Zoom video chats, with Netflix and TikTok as the main sources of entertainment.

Also during this time, the simple three words 'I can't breathe' uttered by George Floyd, murdered by a US policeman, catalyzed worldwide protests against systemic racism and police brutality. And the effects of climate change could no longer be ignored as fires devastated Australia, California, Siberia, Greece, and Turkey.

The profound pressures we face as individuals, organizations, and societies have accelerated the development and adoption of new technologies that are blurring the boundaries between the physical, digital, and biological worlds.

This might all feel like chaos, but there is the hope, possibility, and emergence of something new. We must have the courage and audacity to demand that chaos gives rise to new practices and new ways of leading. We must walk forward into change, even though we don't know what new structures will emerge or even what will survive.

The key actors in this period of transformation will be the next generation of leaders. And they are also the key actors in this book.

So I'm often asked, what is your message to the new generation of leaders? What is this moment about?

I don't really have a single message for you. I spent a year listening to your stories, and I have been moved. As a generation, you are open, curious, and have a lot of wisdom. I think you want to lead with a people-centered lens, in a new, fresh, and innovative way. I think this because so many of you spoke to me about purpose, meaning, diversity and inclusion, and saving the planet.

Don't underestimate how your decisions and actions can make a difference and sometimes impact several generations. Every single one of us can do things – maybe one thing everyday – to change the course of events. My mother's mother risked everything and did this.

I believe that you, the new generation of leaders, don't have any illusions. You have a critical eye – seeing all the complex problems of the world – and yet you remain optimistic. This combination of a critical outlook, optimism, and imagining a better future is driving you to create new opportunities for change and to take the first step.

My father was full of optimism, too. He was more than willing to take the first step, but for him, the lesson of change and transformation was a shocking one. ■

"Ultimately, success depends on having a human connection – both with members of my team and the wider stakeholders, our audience… It's been a learning journey around both how not to lead and how to evolve my style to become an actual leader. Because somebody full of technical knowledge and functional experience ultimately isn't making a difference.

Venetia Bell
Group Chief Sustainability Officer
and Head of Strategy
GIB Asset Management

Chapter 1

THE MYTH OF MANAGING CHANGE

Why we should focus less on the methods of change and more on the people in the change process

My father was seven years old when his family escaped secretly in the middle of the night to prevent Soviet soldiers arresting my grandfather. The family left everything behind and only took what they could carry on their backs.

So I grew up in the USA listening to stories about their life in Uzbekistan. They had lived in a large farm, and my father at age seven had a Karabair – a small and agile steppe horse – and rode behind his father as they inspected the grounds every day. They had an orchard that produced delicious apples, apricots, pears, and cherries in the summer.

In his new life in the US, my father would say: 'These large, flawless fruits in America taste like plastic compared to the fruits from our orchard in Uzbekistan.'

Also he would tell us about his uncles, cousins, and friends who were left behind. He promised that one day he would go back and find the farm, repossess it, and reunite with his family there. My father always stayed optimistic about the possibility, but there seemed little prospect it would actually happen.

Then on August 24 1991, Mikhail Gorbachev resigned as the Communist Party's General Secretary, triggering the speedy collapse of the Soviet Union. Just one week later, on August 31 1991, Uzbekistan declared its independence from the Soviet Union.

Right away my father contacted his family there – 'Don't worry, I'm coming!' – and boarded a flight to the capital Tashkent in the east. He had just retired and took most of his pension money with him to buy back his father's farm and to help his family.

What he found was a shock. The pleasant, fertile farmland of his childhood was replaced by barren earth and poverty. A great deal of poverty. Three months later, he returned to the US, depressed and broke. I'm not sure if he found his father's farm. But we asked him: what did he find?

In the last years of the Soviet era, most Uzbek farmlands were taken over by the government and turned into one vast farm for cotton – considered the white gold of Central Asia. His family members were poor and uneducated – the men, women, and children alike had known nothing but working in the cotton fields. So although it was a time of change and transition, the people there were grappling with immense poverty. They no longer had state help with healthcare, social security or other benefits offered by the Socialist system. And my father was upset that people seemed institutionalized, unmotivated, and largely interested only in spending his American dollars. The thing that stunned him the most, however, was that most Uzbek farm workers looked back at Soviet rule as the good times.

After that traumatic trip to Uzbekistan, my father repeatedly said that we could never return to where we came from. Everything changes, he said, and we would always be refugees of the past without a chance ever to go back to the promised land.

As it turned out, he did go back several times before he passed away – not with the intention of re-finding his home, but simply to help those who stayed there with what little he had.

As my father discovered, everything changes.

This fact is fundamental to the functioning of the universe. The Ancient Greek philosopher, Heraclitus of Ephesus, believed that the only thing constant was change.[1] It's become a cliché, but it's a valuable cliché nevertheless. The Buddha, Heraclitus' Eastern contemporary, also came to the conclusion that nothing was permanent.[2] But he drew an even more useful lesson for us today, suggesting that this is the cause of human suffering: people insisting on continuity (permanence) in a world of constant change (impermanence).

The teachings of both Heraclitus and Buddha challenge us to think about the inevitability of change in every aspect of our lives – personal, professional, and societal. And having spent the past 25 years helping executives, teams, and individuals manage change in *Fortune* 500 companies – with constantly changing markets, technologies, and business landscapes – I understand what they mean.

First, because the human experience requires change at personal, interpersonal, and professional levels. Secondly, because leading a successful business requires change at personal, team, and organizational levels. But thirdly, and most important of all, suffering at all levels of existence comes from holding on to the past, avoiding and fearing change rather than from the change itself.

The implication of holding on, in turn, is that it is not enough for companies simply to survive. It's why the easy axioms such as 'adapt or die', 'innovate or die', 'disrupt or be disrupted', and even the 200-year-old Darwinian Theory of Evolution exhort leaders to take quick action to avoid becoming dinosaurs.

However, these easy axioms are not enough. To thrive in this world today, we need to do more than just change to stay alive and survive. Because the challenge of change is that things will only speed up from now on. A small change to business as usual will not get us to a stable and positive future. Because that stable and positive future itself will change.

In short, leaders need to replace their old thinking about change as a short-term project with a new understanding and a new framework for being resilient and agile in the face of continuous change. This is not just a nice-to-have to build and lead successful companies today. It's crucial for senior leaders to develop these new mindsets and capabilities. If, that is, they're serious about transforming themselves, their teams, and the organization.

Later I'll introduce you to some of the New Leaders of Change, exemplars who are making waves around the world. Because the transformational change we now face requires transformational leaders who see change differently. But first let's look critically at why we've failed to manage change so far.

THE CHALLENGE OF MANAGING CHANGE

Let's be honest: most companies that grew in the 20th century built their success on efficiency, predictability, increased size, and standardization. Many of them, however, have failed, or at best are struggling today to transform or re-invent themselves, to adapt to mid-21st century challenges.

'When machine organizations have tried to engage with the new environment... a very small number of companies have thrived over time,' says Wouter Aghina, a Partner at McKinsey. 'Fewer than 10 per cent of the non-financial S&P 500 companies in 1983 remained in the S&P 500 in 2013. From what we have observed, machine organizations also experience constant internal churn.'

But companies have tried to change, she says.

'According to our research with 1,900 executives, they are adapting their strategy (and their organizational structure) with greater frequency than in the past. Eighty-two per cent of them went through a redesign in the last three years. However, most of these redesign efforts fail – only 23 per cent were implemented successfully.'[3]

This isn't just an occasional, anecdotal problem. Between 2000 and 2014, 52 per cent of companies in the *Fortune* 500 have either gone bankrupt, been acquired, or ceased to exist as a result of accelerated trading and digital disruption[4].

Even when a company recognizes that it isn't managing change well and tries to fix it with the best of intentions, it doesn't always work.

I've had several failed projects in traditional organizational settings in the development of agile teams.

A common scenario is that the interface between application development and operational teams, their customers, and their partners is not working well. Hand-offs and accountabilities are not properly defined. There are huge backlogs and team morale is low.

This is when outside consultants are called in. After a little work, everyone is given the vision of creating agile and multidisciplinary teams to address the issues they are facing. After careful planning and design, these agile teams are launched. Their launch is communicated and celebrated.

After six months, however, the program fails. The external consultants are called in – again – to assess what went wrong.

Here's what they discover – that the key factors that led to failure are predictable. Usually it is some combination of the following, if not all of them:

- **Traditional organizations are structured hierarchically** and rely on a vertical chain of command, with leaders at the top and many layers of management underneath. Agility requires flatter organizations that are networked and enable collaboration across boundaries.

- **Managers from different departments continue to measure team members with traditional KPIs** (key performance indicators) that instigate and proliferate siloed behaviors. They do not cultivate team behaviors that lead to 'being agile', such as cross-functional collaboration, teamwork, transparency, and inclusivity.

- **Managers prevent their teams sharing important project data** with partners and customers, so half the team members don't have the right information.

- **Managers from different functional departments cannot agree on the budget allocations** for the agile team's requirements. Decisions continue to go upward to the management rather than empowering teams to make decisions.

Jayson Noland of IT start-up Cloudflare has observed that traditional companies built for bureaucracy, hierarchy, centralized information flow, and siloed functions are frustrating for the new generation of leaders. 'The organizational charts in traditional companies are built in a way that makes it really hard to be a young and upcoming leader,' he says.

'They are composed of large teams of 50-100 people, so there are few opportunities. The positions tend to be tenure-based, so you have to be in the company for 10+ years and of a certain age and have a certain degree before you get offered a leadership position. And it gets really political.'

Start-ups, he says, tend to handle this better – thanks to small, agile teams. 'In the start-up world, there are a bunch of little teams, you know, four or five-person teams.' Traditional organizations, on the other hand, with 20th century business operating models – strategy, structure, culture, and leadership – are not set up for success in 21st century.

Having spent 25 years in and around organizational change, it is clear to me that many new generation leaders are frustrated with hierarchies, top-down power, and controls. These impede people's ability to voice views, and box them into roles that limit their abilities and creativity. And most importantly, they miss out on leveraging the human potential, as well as the potential of new digital technologies. So the key challenge is how to rethink and reconfigure organizations and leadership mindset to apply 21st century thinking to 21st century opportunities.

We'll come back to agile teams later, but why do so many companies fail at change? Why don't leaders in traditional companies do something before the situation becomes so dire that the only options are lay-offs, radical cost cutting, and downsizing?

It's an unfortunate fact that companies' change and transformation programs have a dismal track record. In 1995, Harvard Business School professor John Kotter claimed that 50-70 per cent of large-scale change programs did not achieve their intended outcomes. This was often due to employees' attitudes and management misalignment with the change program, he said. And virtually every survey in the last 25 years has shown similar results.

The question still remains: why do they fail? Often people simply shrug. The opportunity for disruption, they say, picking that moment, is a lot easier to see with hindsight. The leaders of the time simply didn't see the threat that was happening, goes the excuse. They didn't recognize the patterns. They didn't identify their options.

Having witnessed and indeed played a part in so many cases of change that fails, I can rule out these excuses. The blind leader or the under-resourced leadership team are fallacies. As a generalization they are simply not true.

The *Fortune* 500 companies I worked with had very competent strategy teams that worked closely with the big consulting firms – Accenture, McKinsey, Bain, Boston Consulting Group, and so on. Their leadership teams spent many hours participating actively in strategy sessions with strategy experts, poring over hundreds of pages of data and PowerPoint presentations.

Table 1: The key reasons why change programs fail

1. POLITICS AND FEAR OF CANNIBALIZING EXISTING BUSINESS

For many executives, adopting new product, services, and delivery models would potentially cannibalize profitable revenue streams. Under the pressure of meeting quarterly results and meeting financial expectations, making the change was never a realistic option.

In addition, discussions with the leaders who have been growing and managing that business line for 25+ years were highly political.

2. COST OF DIGITIZATION

For many traditional companies with obsolete legacy IT infrastructure, it would cost too much money and disruption to modernize.

3. TALENT AND SKILLS GAP

Many traditional companies and leadership teams are held back by a talent gap – a gap in understanding and experience of new technologies such as artificial intelligence (AI), machine learning, data analytics, and robotics – as well as a skills gap – a gap in skills in transformation, change, leadership, agile methods and practices, collaboration, and innovation. It is clear the 20th century capabilities will not lead to success in the 21st century environment.

4. FEAR OF NEW TECHNOLOGY AND CHANGE

I have watched senior executives being reluctant to embrace digital transformation due to uncertainty and fear about new technologies. The multiple layers of technology and platform modernization are complex and massive. To most executives who have little knowledge and information about new technologies, digital transformation is perceived as a minefield.

5. BUREAUCRACY, HIERARCHY, AND TOP-DOWN CONTROL

Many organizations fail to change, transform, and behave in an agile way because of organizational complexity – they are burdened with cumbersome processes, controlling mechanisms, layers of hierarchy, silos.

6. INWARD-LOOKING

I have witnessed many organizations spend millions on market/customer/competitive data collection and at the end totally ignore its implications for their change and transformation strategy.

The conversations often center around internal efficiency, productivity, and cost-cutting measures, versus customers, innovations, and competitive advantage. The transformation process is hampered by a culture of internal focus – the innovation process is inside-out rather than outside-in.

Most of the time they followed a good process. Someone set up a Transformation Program Office with internal resources, strategy consultants, and an executive committee, including senior members of the leadership team. Then, within a year, the transformation agenda had been turned into a massive workforce and cost optimization program.

And yet many still failed. Looking at some of the key reasons for the failure of change programs from my own experience, it's clear: problems can be varied and complicated. Just take a look at Table 1.

In short, many of the reasons behind failure to change are associated with the fact that companies are much larger today than they have ever been.

Why? Of course, the corporate mantra has almost always been big is beautiful. The thing is, business leaders and founders don't start out to create massively complex organizations. Often it just happens, over years or decades. One day you realize your small, agile organization has layers of bureaucratic structures, with multiple management layers, cumbersome legacy processes and systems, slow decision approval processes, and very high costs.

However, there is one thing that's very clear. One of the challenges inherent in working in large organizations is spending too much time on the internal activities that have no impact on customer success, on growth or on competitive advantage. From my own experience, probably almost 30-40 per cent of executives' time is spent on these internal activities. And there's a price to pay.

I have watched senior leaders and skilled transformation directors become intimidated in the face of the rapid disruption, uncertainty, and exponential change cascading through large and highly bureaucratic organizations.

When a situation like this arises, where an organization grows so complex that it's sabotaging its own agility and resilience, it's hard for even the simplest of change management programs to rectify. And even the most skilled influencer in such a situation can find change difficult.

When you want a change program to begin, for example, sometimes transformation directors help executives to define the starting point, or the context that requires the change. And we are adept, aren't we, at describing the context in which change is required – borrowing military acronyms, for example, like VUCA (Volatile, Uncertain, Complex, and Ambiguous), or mathematical terms such as exponential (meaning a very rapid increase or a sharp and fast expansion) to describe this new reality. But understanding the context isn't enough. We are still struggling to come up with new ways of making change happen.

Another tactic when leaders want to initiate change is to describe the end state, or the benefits of making the change. In most cases, major organizational change initiatives fail outright or do not achieve their desired objectives and the benefits of change. Given the poor success rate of change and transformation programs, many leaders are hesitant to act decisively and offer a clean definition of the end state and what is required to get there.

One reason some executives offer for resisting change is that they recognize, logically, the need to change, but they are not confident about its return on investment. Want proof? Incredibly, while 96 per cent of organizations report they are undergoing business transformations, only 47 per cent expect to realize sustainable value from those efforts, according to one important KPMG Global Transformation study.[5]

So the implication of this is all too clear: managing change in large organizations is hard. I have had a front-row seat and often a driving seat helping leaders, teams, and individuals so I can attest to the challenges of making change happen and trying to manage the change process. I can attest to the fact that there are many reasons change programs fail. In fact, when you look into this, you find hundreds of popular books and thousands of scholarly articles analyzing why change efforts fail, with many researchers and scholars recommending that we make subtle or even not so subtle revisions to the current practices and processes of change management.

However, I would like to ask a more fundamental question: are the 20th century methods of change management that exist today appropriate for the challenges we face in the 21st century? Do we, in fact, need to focus less on the methods and structures of change and more on the people leading change and the people impacted by it?

WHY DO CURRENT MODELS OF CHANGE FAIL?

Thinking about whether the process of change management is up to the job for a moment, the recent trends describing organizations as complex systems and the subsequent calls for disruptive strategies suggest we need to embrace a far more substantial shift from conventional change management than we have so far dared. When change tests the agility, adaptability, and resilience not only of institutions, but also communities and individuals as well, you begin to realize – whether you work in a start-up or traditional business – the challenge today is to succeed in a world of extreme chaos.

This becomes a challenge when you actually study the most popular models of change management still taught today, most of which were developed in the 20th century, mostly in the West, and most of which share common characteristics. They define change as a single three-stage process involving unfreezing or initiating, changing or transitioning, and then refreezing or stabilizing. These are mostly variations of the three-stage model devised in 1947 by Kurt Lewin, one of the founders of modern social psychology. And while it became the basis for many later models, it has also been widely criticized, notably by Rosabeth Moss Kanter at Harvard Business School.

In her book *The Challenge of Organizational Change* (1992) her comments on Lewin's three-stage model capture the essence of why we need to redefine how change happens in the 21st century.

'This quaintly linear and static conception – the organization as an ice cube – is so wildly inappropriate that it is difficult to see why it has not only survived but prospered... Suffice it to say here, first, that organizations are never frozen, much less refrozen, but are fluid entities with many "personalities". Second, to the extent that there are stages, they overlap and interpenetrate one another in important ways.'

It's another Harvard Business School professor, John Kotter, who's now widely regarded as the foremost authority on leading change and in his now classic *Leading Change* (1996), built on with a set of follow-up titles, he sets out what he describes as a simple, actionable, eight-step process:

1. Establish a **sense of urgency**.
2. Form a powerful **guiding coalition**.
3. **Create a vision**.
4. **Communicate the vision**.
5. **Empower others** to act on the vision.
6. Plan for and create **short-term wins**.

7. **Consolidate improvements** and produce still more change.
8. **Institutionalize** new approaches.

This eight-step model is obviously more complex and comprehensive than earlier models. However, its underpinning assumptions continue to exemplify the planned, linear, and controlled style of change management. For example, change is still seen as a one-off event with a defined beginning and a successful end that is reached by following each of the eight steps in a linear order.

Like Lewin before him, Kotter's underlying assumption is that change is linear, incremental, evolutionary, and subject to the reassuring law of cause and effect. Ultimately, his work implies that the outcome from change programs is predictable and can be managed.

We like linear stages, though. Traditional organizations and leaders really like them, because the process has a beginning and an ending. If you start with stage one, and you move on through stage eight, you think you're done. Your organization, employees, and customers will be transformed. As a leader, you will no longer have to think about change and transformation. But this is not true in today's business context, where changes are continuous and accelerate exponentially. We need to be able to live with change, to adopt and thrive with change, both personally and organizationally.

There's an even more worrying aspect to Kotter's model for the business world today. His model assumes that the vision for change, a sense of urgency and empowerment, can only come from top leadership down. It seems to exclude informal, lateral, and bottom-up leadership – all the intrapreneurs who are shaking up traditional organizations. Unfortunately this is a process that might disempower employees who can feel like pawns on a leadership chessboard.

Today, innovation can come from anyone and anywhere. Because everyone is digitally connected, many people, inside and outside the organization, expect to be involved in decisions that impact current practices. In digital native companies such as Google, Facebook, and Spotify, equal importance is given to bottom-up innovation and change. Many transformative ideas are initiated by employees, as opposed to top-down transformation fueled by leaders.

In this new situation, the hierarchy and silos created in the traditional organizations can inhibit change, collaboration, and agility – and even create mistrust. We need to revisit the linear models of change where all the predetermined phases of change occur in sequence. The approach depends on predictable processes and experience. The method is standardized, repeatable, and the same for all change projects. This is not effective for today's volatile, ambiguous, connected, fast, complex digital business context. It is cumbersome, restrictive, and not designed for the new digital era of speed.

The reality is that leading change is messy – it's not just top-down versus bottom-up. It involves a mixed bag of practices, experiments, and shifts in behaviors, depending on the context. In some contexts, leaders set the parameters for the organization from the top – on strategic decisions, brand vision, purpose, and goals. In other contexts, they engage employees, customers, and other stakeholders in a conversation about the best way to accelerate change, in order to earn their commitment and engagement.

What we've seen in the 21st century and what I argue for here is to give greater consideration to the more people-centric models of organization, leadership, and change that are evolving. We need to recognize that – increasingly – change cannot be driven only from the top, but can also emerge in an organic, bottom-up fashion from the day-to-day actions of everyone in the organization. And – counter-intuitively, perhaps – that depends on support from leaders. We need leaders who emphasize a culture of creativity, innovation, entrepreneurship, and empowerment.

How do linear models fit into the VUCA change environment of the 21st century?

The quick answer: actually, not at all.

WE'RE STILL ROOTED IN 20th CENTURY THINKING

I can confirm that, in my 25+ years of experience, I have yet to participate in or observe a serious change program that followed a simple, linear, top-down approach. That is because organizations are not simple, and change has complex, systemic effects that cannot be constrained in a linear model. You cannot manage the change process – there will be unintended consequences that cannot be planned for or controlled. In today's complex environment, we need leaders who can embrace change, who can work across silos, and who are adaptable – not leaders who set out to manage change according to predefined methods.

My argument in *The New Leaders of Change* is that we need to focus less on the linear step-wise methods of managing change and more on the people involved in the process and on their very real concerns and contributions. If it isn't already, the Zeitgeist will soon be to measure everything against whether it helps people, the planet, and our wider purpose, rather than just profit.

In reverse order, then, increasingly we are focusing on a life that matters and work that has meaning. For many of us that is connected with the second element: serving the planet and ensuring the sustainability of our foothold here. And finally we are on a journey towards becoming more humane, more aware of our interdependency with the environment, the interconnectedness of people and societies around the world. By taking a people-centric view, leaders have a chance to better lead change and transformation successfully in this hyperconnected, global, and digital era.

But before we can explore the implications of people-centered change and fully and truly challenge our approach to change, we first need to step back. We need to re-evaluate the underlying assumptions and beliefs that govern today's traditional organizations and the traditional change management approaches we have so far taken. In other words, before we can accept the need to change our mindset and approach to change, we must understand where our thinking, assumptions, and beliefs about change came from.

Because what's clear is that we are facing a paradigm shift – a new understanding when it comes to organizations, leadership, change, and transformation.

What's astonishing here is that our assumptions and beliefs about change can be traced back to revolutions in science and economics over the past couple centuries – right back to the First and Second Industrial Revolutions. The First Industrial Revolution used water and steam power to mechanize production in the 18th century; the Second used electric power to create mass production in the 19th century. And it was both these revolutions combined that shaped the Western world and established ways of thinking about the world, the position of everyone in that world, and – critically – about the nature of management.

For example, it was the steam and railway revolution of the mid-19th century that led to the line-and-staff model of people management, the emergence of professionally managed firms with a clear hierarchical structure, and industrial factories. These in turn gave rise to the relatively new economic system we call capitalism that valued profits for the owners above people and environment.

Later the steel and electricity revolution of late 19th and early 20th centuries prompted workflow optimization, efficiency, and productivity based on a mechanistic view of organizations and people as machines. The research underpinning this came to be known as scientific management and its principles were captured in print by Frederick Winslow Taylor, a mechanical engineer, in 1911. (Frighteningly, the book was described as the most influential management book of the 20th century by the American Academy of Management.)

Shortly afterwards Henri Fayol, a French mining engineer, published General and Industrial Administration in 1916, based on much the same thinking. Planning, organizing, commanding, and control were key, he said.

The underlying assumption of scientific management was that people, like machines, could be standardized, measured, and controlled to increase productivity. To managers like Taylor and Fayol, the birth of the people/machine factory was accompanied by clearly defined roles and tasks, and there were precise metrics for efficiency and productivity. Mistakes could easily be identified and eliminated. And if mistakes did occur, people could be identified, blamed, and punished. Soon a predictable and reassuringly linear environment was built and mass production manufacturing became the norm.

Then the automobile and oil revolution of the mid-20th century gave rise to massive corporations to support production, marketing, and sales of different products to different customer segments. These corporations evolved into multi-divisional, mass-production firms with autonomous divisions under central strategic direction. In the corporate system, the customer became a thing to be manipulated (rather than a person with whom the corporation had a relationship) to buy the products and services generated by the system. Similarly, the employees were treated as human resources, resources that could be controlled, exploited, and discarded as necessary.

For much of the 20th century, this worked well enough. In a stable world like that of the 1950s and 1960s, with strong demand, established firms in control of the marketplace could get away with manipulating customers and exploiting the employees. But the model eventually led to poor quality and service, low worker morale and involvement, lack of co-operation, and political games among managers.

The next iterations of the modern corporate model gave rise to total quality management, as well as models of organizational culture and organizational learning, among other things. These movements were a step in the right direction. They encouraged managers to involve employees at all levels – not only to improve products and processes, but also to accelerate efficiency and productivity. However, even these movements did not change the underlying scientific management paradigm – that what matters can be measured and what can't be measured doesn't matter. They only put in place processes to correct any dysfunctions and to restabilize the corporate structure.

What else is tainted with the principles of scientific management? Well, many of the operational change processes of the late 20th century, such as business process engineering, total quality management, and ISO 9000, owe much to principles of scientific management.

WHY DO THESE THEORIES MATTER TODAY?

Now you might think that these 19th and 20th century management theories have little relevance for us today. And you're right. But I assure you this constellation of beliefs, values, and practices is shaping organizational and management operating models even now. So much so that to ask what part Taylor and Fayol had in shaping today's management practices is like asking what influence did Newton and Einstein have on physics. Scientific management permeates virtually all current management thinking, either visibly and explicitly or invisibly and implicitly.

The organization-as-a-machine metaphor is ubiquitous. It determines our perceptions, ways of working, expectations, and our mental models about organization, leadership, change, and success. Our everyday language is infused with it: 'well oiled machine', 'on autopilot', 'firing on all cylinders'. We speak of the need to 're-engineer' processes to increase 'efficiency and reliability'. We seek 'maximum utilization of human resources'.

It is clear that these models are no longer adequate. They are built for environments that are stable and certain, where decisions are made at the top and communicated via a centralized chain of command, where departments operate as standalone. Today's environment, however, is volatile, uncertain, complex, and ambiguous. Companies and leaders are solving the challenges of innovation, creativity, speed, collaboration, and exponential change.

Frankly, too many analysts still claim the principles of scientific management offer the most significant theory of management, while what's come to be known as human relations – which at least considers workers to be human beings – is mere window dressing.

I disagree. And I put it to you that it's no wonder so many young people today feel that 20th century business and 20th century governments aren't working for us any longer. It's why they want to build 21st century solutions for 21st century problems.

A PEOPLE-CENTERED APPROACH TO CHANGE

'I was trained in all the traditional change tools like stakeholder analysis, change impact assessment, and change communication plan,' says Kim Bertz, now Senior Vice President, Workplace Services & Experience, at Wells Fargo, the US financial services company.

'However, I quickly realized that in a complex change and transformation program, the role of change consultant can be anything and everything. During a crisis in the program, all the change-related analysis did not really help the situation. It was more about being nimble and understanding the context and who is on point for what, versus having a well structured and managed change plan.

'What worked for me was to really listen and study what is really going on. It was all about understanding the human needs – understanding the different audiences and stakeholders.' And she pauses, reflecting on the simplicity of it.

'When I think about what I do now, these are the most critical skills to manage change – agility to move fast. To do that you need to understand the context, know who is on point for what, and understand the needs and feelings of the key stakeholders.'

Bertz is not alone in her discoveries. Venetia Bell, in her first leadership position, perceived her role very much from a technical and functional perspective, exemplifying the core tenets of scientific management.

'I was leading a very technical team,' she says. 'I was running the short-term forecasts team at the Bank of England, doing lots of technical analysis, and my first leadership role was very much technical. It was lots of research, it was trying to really make a contribution to the literature and to important weighty economic topics.'

Having joined the Bank of England, the UK's central bank, as Deputy to the Chief Operating Officer, she worked mainly in monetary analysis. In other words, she was involved with forming and implementing the bank's strategic plan. And she saw the role of leader as managing the technical functions of the team, not so much the people.

'I approached it very much from that technical and functional perspective and it didn't turn out too well,' she says, grimacing at the recollection.

Her big lesson was to bring the human element into her approach. 'I learned there are far more important aspects to leadership than functional knowledge and technical experiences,' she says. 'That role was a journey around people, collaboration, and seeing the whole picture from various stakeholder perspectives.'

What turned the role around, I ask. What made it successful for her?

'Ultimately, success depended on having a human connection – both with members of my team and the wider stakeholders, our audience.'

I notice how she describes the role as a journey. 'It was a learning journey around both how not to lead and how to evolve my style to become an actual leader. Somebody full of technical knowledge and functional experience ultimately isn't making a difference.'

It's clear that people-centered leadership gives new perspectives on how to lead, how to motivate and engage people for successful business results. At the same time, however, it reveals new challenges. A human-centered approach takes us away from linear, technocratic and hierarchical models of leadership and change toward cultivating engagement, connection, and collaboration with the people we work with and the stakeholders we impact.

At the Bank of England, Bell came face to face with these challenges.

'I guess there was a moment of realization when I was dealing with one important external stakeholder, the Office for National Statistics here in the UK,' she says. 'My team had discovered some issues with the data and was taking a very technocratic approach to solving the problem.' The team identified the issues and what needed to be done to improve them, but failed to look at the bigger picture – the impact on the Bank as a whole.

'We were very much going in with that technical lens and totally failing to see the wider pressures on the organization and how criticism from us would seriously damage its external reputation, and how that was playing into their concerns and their positioning.' It was a tough lesson.

'We learned about the importance of discussing the issues with them and working them out and finding a collaborative solution, rather than a more adversarial approach that was grounded in the technical content.'

Now Head of Strategy at GIB Asset Management, Bell has overall responsibility for devising and implementing company strategy and in 2017 she was named one of Management Today's 35 Women Under 35. Clearly her early leadership lessons worked out.

Bringing in the human element, as Bell has done, is vital in all areas of leadership, it seems to me, especially where change is concerned. Now, for the first time, we're really beginning to hear a new vocabulary in common use by today's leaders – 'collaboration', 'listening', 'relationships', 'understanding', 'bringing stakeholders with you willingly', rather than 'managing' or convincing them to follow a step-wise process.

'My main wish for the next generation of leaders is around authenticity and sensitivity,' says Bell, 'and allowing themselves to flourish as they grow into leadership and not letting that be crushed out of them by all the people, systems, hierarchy, and the way current top-down organizations are.'

She's optimistic for the future, it seems, and believes that newly emerging leaders have a chance of changing things – but only if they hang on to their beliefs and values.

'I hope the next generation will have more confidence in themselves and do not feel they have to compromise and conform to the *status quo*,' she says.

Is that likely?

'I think sometimes people do make compromises about who they are because they feel that they need to conform in a particular way. Life, success, career is not like an elevator where you've got to do things in a particular linear way – this way and only this way to the top. I just don't believe that is the case – life is not like an elevator.'

Bell's language is nothing like the language of scientific management. And it's focused entirely on the people she works with and her hopes for their future.

'We all do things in our own different ways, learn at different rates, so this is a learning journey.' That journey word again. 'And it doesn't matter where you are heading,' she says. 'Try to do your very best in the world.'

Bell's approach is refreshing because the times we are living in now are unlike any other. The Third and now the Fourth Industrial Revolutions are characterized by changes that first appeared gradual, but that suddenly and unexpectedly have become explosive (see Table 2). This is an era that's been described – not for nothing – as the Exponential Era[6], notably by Peter Diamandis, Founder of the X-Prize foundation, and the science writer Steven Kotler. 'The human brain,' they say, 'is not wired to think in exponential terms.'

Isn't that a bit of an exaggeration? Well, not according to Adrian Locher, CEO and Founder of Merantix, a German software studio focused on artificial intelligence.

'We believe artificial intelligence and machine learning are the most

Table 2: The four industrial revolutions heralding the emergence of digital technologies

First Industrial Revolution	*Mid-18th to early 19th century*
Mechanization and replacement of agriculture by industry as primary economy	
Second Industrial Revolution	*Mid-19th to early 20th century*
Emergence of electricity, gas and oil industries	
Third Industrial Revolution	*Mid-late 20th century*
Electronics, telecommunications, computing, nuclear power	
Fourth Industrial Revolution	*Late 20th to 21st century*
Internet and digital technologies including AI, machine learning, and virtual reality	

important and impactful technologies of the 21st century so far. To us it's a general-purpose technology much like steam, electricity, software, or the internet itself. And we believe due to its nature – augmenting and automating human decision-making with higher accuracy – it will have an even bigger impact on the world.'

He's not alone in his assessment. 'We are only seeing the tip of the iceberg in what these technologies can do for us, our businesses and society at large,' says Martin Baart, CEO of Ecoligo, which enables businesses in emerging markets to better use solar energy. And he goes further.

'What these technologies will bring us and how they will affect our future lives is beyond comprehension.' He shakes his head at the magnitude of it all.

'In the past, technology came along and made an existing concept better. Sending email was better then sending a fax, was better then sending a letter,' he says. These were marginal improvements on the same way of doing things. Now, the new technologies are allowing us to do things in completely different ways and they all work together. With every improvement, in every single technology, we see an exponential growth of their collective effects.

'For traditional businesses that have not understood this and have not yet adjusted their traditional operating models, it will soon be very difficult to adjust,' he says.

Why?

'The longer you wait, the bigger your adjustment will be. Also, you will lose the experience of applying new technologies to your business model, so that competitors who do will have gained a significant advantage.'

But can't companies just plan ahead for these technological changes? Build an emerging technology roadmap into their strategies?

Baart thinks not. 'The days of long-term planning, preparation, implementation, and the slow adoption of technology is over. The technologies themselves arrive much faster than we can even plan. So we have to be able to change and adapt quickly to whatever is changing around us.'

There's something else we have to accept, too, he says. 'We have to accept that the changes we require could be rather radical, even to the extent of completely changing a business or business model. And not only the number of things that are changing, but their impact as well will increase.'

What does that mean for business and for leaders, then?

'As a consequence in business we must implement structures, processes, and a culture that can be changed quickly, and especially we need to allow for fast innovation and decision processes. At Ecoligo, we innovate freely of any constraints of technologies,' he says. 'We think about which cool idea could help us to get better at what we do. And we imagine this without any technological constraint. These bold ideas – that may sound very ridiculous or unrealistic at first – are then mapped out. And based on this we look at which technologies could help us to achieve their implementation.'

Building on Locher and Baart's vision of technology as a key driver of speed when it comes to leading change, I want to add a different element to consider: hyperconnectivity.[7] Because where new technology is concerned, everything can now connect with everything else. And that brings its own rewards and challenges.

The move towards hyperconnectivity is fueled by the simultaneous emergence of the Internet of Things (IOT), big data, machine and deep learning, augmented and virtual reality, mobile communication networks and digitization, among many other things. And with everything hooked together, it revolutionizes access to knowledge, education, and relationships, for sure. But it also revises dramatically the nature of work, it brings into question the value of travel, the supply chain, food production – the list is endless. So hyperconnectivity is not a unique technology platform as such – it's socio-cultural change on a grand scale. Organizations, industries, governments, and people will have no choice but to change and adapt.

In the context of this book and you, the New Leaders of Change, it makes sense to take hyperconnectivity seriously, but from a distinctly human viewpoint. Through a human lens, there's no doubt that technology will be a profound tool to help us all understand people's experience – their values, needs, expectations, and desires, for example. But hyperconnectivity itself will be woven into the fabric of human experience more and more. And the most successful businesses will be those that can integrate their hypernetworks with humanistic values. Those who can engage people – customers, employees, partners, and a wider general public – to co-create a new course for the future.

So to truly bring a human touch to the Fourth Industrial Revolution, the hyperconnected enterprise must be rooted in purpose, collaboration, trust, and value for all stakeholders. Networks, after all, are very human things. But that's a subject for another book.

If, as Diamandis and Kotler say, we are not wired for this hyperconnected, exponential era, then how are we as humans going to keep up? How are individuals and organizations to prepare for changes of the magnitude and impact of all the new digital technologies? How can we take advantage of the opportunities and thwart the threats facing us in this Exponential Era?

First, we need to acknowledge – again – that change and the transformation process are hard, messy, and non-linear. It requires new forms of collaboration, and new types of organizations that can respond to complexity, rapid change, and uncertainty. But we also need to recognize that our ability to change and adapt can be the unlocking mechanisms for creativity, resilience, and success. Now, more than ever, we need a big shift in our mindset about change.

So how do we shift our mindset from managing change as a set of distinct projects with a beginning and an end to a mindset where change is continuous, where change is 'business as usual; it is what we do'.

Some of us are already shifting. Because it's the next generation of leaders who most are disrupting what it means to be a leader in the 21st century. They are fueling a movement towards more purpose-driven leadership based on making a difference versus just earning a paycheck.[8] They want to work for inspirational companies who no longer believe that financial results are the only or primary measure of success. They want to work for companies that make a positive impact on the planet, societies, customers, and the people who work with them.

So where do we start when it comes to exploring people-centered change? Where do we go from here?

One way of understanding an organization and change might be as a human process. The people-centered lens will give us a view of the organization not as a machine but as an ever shifting, evolving, and changing set of people, ideas, and relationships. And the core focus is not 'to be in control', but on relationships, the quality of conversations, engagement and collaboration.

When you remove unrealistic expectations of control, predictability, and stability, there is an opening for curiosity, empathy, discovery, experimentation, learning, risk-taking, and reflection.

In some ways, however, this is a false way of looking at it. Because people have always been at the center of any kind of change. Even in linear change models, it's always people who drive change. The ultimate objective of all business has always been about people for people – customers, employees, investors, partners, and communities. Every new innovation and every new technology is created by people, or operated by people. Creativity is only ever brought into a project by people. As we remove people from business, we remove the human touch and we dehumanize organizations and the people involved.

It's just that the linear, stage-focused models prescribe predictable steps, whether that's three, six or eight. And that creates a problem. First, the number itself gives you the illusion of having predictable outcomes through each step. And secondly, because it's a finite process with a limited number of steps, at the end of the process the assumption is that the change has finished. Everybody's transformed. The culture has changed. The organization works differently. But we all know that this just isn't true. The reality is that change never stops. Change is constant. Change is about people. Change can involve tough conversations. Change can be messy.

PUT PEOPLE AT THE HEART OF CHANGE

What the new research here in *The New Leaders of Change* highlights, and what my own theory of people-centered leadership captures as a result, is that if we put people very clearly at the center of the change process – versus the way it is with linear steps, where people are an afterthought – we can better understand what motivates people, what drives creativity and innovation, and how we can support people during times of change, stress, or disruption. And when I say people, I'm talking about all the key stakeholders that will be affected by the change. Customers will almost always be impacted, but also employees, partners, communities, or even society as a whole. To be frank, they all are involved anyway, often by default, so let's consciously bring people into the center and engage them from the beginning, bringing their collective knowledge, experience, ideas, passion, and energy into the change process.

Perhaps part of the challenge is that change makes many people feel uncomfortable. Change is a stress amplifier. Part of the brain – the amygdala – interprets change as a threat and releases the hormones for fear, anxiety, and stress. And so the only way to avoid stress and anxiety, to my way of thinking, is to put the people at the heart of the change process, integrating those who will be affected into the process of co-designing the change. Co-creating solutions and leading the implementation can inspire a movement around the change.

A deep understanding of the motivations, expectations, needs, and emotions of the people impacted by change requires a degree of empathizing at the emotional and cognitive levels. The new generation of leaders in my research emphasize the importance of empathy – they tell many stories about how an ability to empathize helped them manage relationships with others and orient them towards solutions.

There's a challenge with this, of course. Shifting the lens from steps in a process to working with people at the center will be messier. I'm not promising that 'by the end of step eight, you're going to have a transformed organization' or 'all the people are going to change'. That doesn't happen anyway, but let that stand for a moment. What people will inevitably ask is why should I follow you as a leader? What's your vision? What's your purpose? What's our purpose? Where's the passion pulling me towards that future? In the past we perhaps haven't thought enough about this and we really need to.

So it's really a change in focus and practices that I'm advocating. A theory of people-centered leadership refocuses our minds on the people involved in change, moderating the processes involved and inspiring people to get involved and undertake the change that's needed.

WHAT DOES IT MEAN TO BE PEOPLE-CENTERED?

This change of focus raises a number of specific questions. How do you become more obviously people-centered? How do you involve people in change? How do you engage people? There are other questions, too. Leaders at the early and not-so-early stages of their professional lives often ask for long-term advice. For example, how can you build your career as a people-centered leader?

My answer to all of these questions begins with really looking at yourself, and reflecting on your leadership style. What is your vision for your leadership? Your purpose? What are the values that guide your decisions and actions? And then really to challenge yourself: are they humanistic? Do you consider the impact of your actions on people and planet as well as business?

One way of exploring this is to ask what does your leadership look like on a daily basis? When you reflect on it, what do you most worry about? Do you think about individual and team performance, deadlines, projects, status reports? Or do you think about the needs of the people who make the work actually happen? Do you seek to understand what makes people thrive, what drives creativity and problem-solving in the company, and how you can support people during times of change, stress, or disruption?

Because being people-centered is not an intellectual, theoretical exercise. It's hard, deep thinking, but it's not something you need a degree in. It's really about how you feel within yourself. How you feel about working with, engaging with, and forming relationships with people.

So become more aware of your assumptions, your pre-conceived ideas, and your ready judgments. Next time you are in a conversation with someone whose views and beliefs differ from yours, practice empathy by having an open, curious conversation without judgment. Reflect on the experience – what did you learn? Were you able to understand their point-of-view? Did you discover something surprising? Start there.

After 25 years of consulting and coaching executives of Fortune 500 companies globally, I can say this: in looking for better ways to lead and manage change, we can take inspiration from you, from the next generation of leaders. You are beginning to stand out as leaders of change at the center of our economic, social, and political systems. You are empathetic and inclusive leaders who put people at the center, create a sense of belonging, and build deep purpose and engagement not only in their organizations but also throughout the corporate ecosystem. They are well equipped to manage the realities of exponential change that we face in the 21st century.

What remains to address, then, is the central question at the heart of this book: exactly what do the New Leaders of Change look like today? And how will they change themselves, their businesses, and the world?

Let's start with my granddaughter. ■

The NEW LEADERS of CHANGE

PART II: CHARACTERISTICS

NEW LEADERSHIP ATTRIBUTES

"There is no single way that Google manages internal change, like a reorganization. There is no change methodology that defines the change road map, how to get to the end-state most effectively. Because at Google, we often don't have a static end-state we're looking for; we need to maintain a fluidity in our structures to support the pace of our business.

Banks Baker
Head of Global Partnerships (Search Content)
Google

Chapter 2

LEARNING TO LEAD EXPONENTIAL CHANGE

In search of agility and innovation

I became a grandmother in April 2017 and it changed my life. Watching my granddaughter grow up is teaching me many lessons about life and what it means to be a human. And I think they are lessons business needs to learn too.

As we try to proactively understand the impact of VUCA – those volatile, uncertain, complex, and ambiguous factors facing business – and to prepare defensive solutions, there's a question I can't help asking. How can we plan for uncertainty and ambiguity? How do we reinvent our businesses in a radically new way – what some might call engaging in creative destruction – before we are destroyed by the competition?

Playing with my granddaughter, I am always surprised how she is delighted by ambiguity, uncertainty and even destruction – it is essential to her play and playfulness.

When she is uncertain, she becomes inquisitive and asks a million questions.

When she is in an ambiguous situation, she becomes intensely curious to explore the unknown, experiment with it, and make sense out of it.

And when we finally complete the construction of a complicated Lego design at home, or a sandcastle on the beach, she takes a moment to observe and be proud of our accomplishments. And then, with a look of mischief and delight, she engages in an act of destruction, laughing the whole time, perhaps at the surprised horror of my expression. She is not afraid to disrupt, to be curious, to be creative. And she is constantly ready to re-engage!

What can we learn from how children play? First we need to unlearn some of the socialization, the grooming, and the training that dampened our own creativity, curiosity, and exploration. Then we need to relearn these very human skills that are so necessary to succeed in the VUCA business environment where change is continuous and exponential.

You, the new generation of leaders, are curious about the dynamics of change, uncertainty, and ambiguity. You are more willing to disrupt the *status quo* and explore new opportunities with optimism, curiosity, and excitement. As a result, you are forging new types of solutions and creating new ways forward for yourselves and for your businesses.

So here's the challenge for all of us: now is the time to challenge, assess, and re-assess our deeply ingrained assumptions, beliefs and practices about how we create value, success, and growth. There has never been a better opportunity nor a need to get out of our comfort zone, embrace big ideas, and make an impact.

Martin Baart, CEO of Ecoligo, which enables businesses in emerging markets to use solar energy, is passionate about leading in a people-centric and agile way.

'I don't care who gets credit – I want to provide the best solution,' he says. 'I have big ideas. Everyone has. I put them into action.'

He puts it in a very simple way. 'I lead by example.'

WHAT DOES 'LEAD BY EXAMPLE' MEAN?

For many who say something like 'I lead by example', you have to question whether they really mean it. But Baart began his career in a large, traditional engineering company before joining a start-up and finally starting his own company. And he is someone with ambitions – his LinkedIn tagline is clear: 'Saving the planet as the CEO of Ecoligo'.

Baart believes it's tough for traditional companies to adopt more agile practices and make change happen more rapidly. 'I think systemic change will just take so long in traditional organizations that change programs never have a chance to succeed,' he says. 'Because, at the end of the day, they want to see results at a quarterly basis, which is the old paradigm.' And when yesterday's executives want to see results quarterly, what happens if results don't come? The budget for those programs is cut, he says.

'The second reason is that our externalities are changing much faster that we can design, develop, and implement programs for changing huge numbers of people at many levels. It will usually take six months to set up a program and 12 months to roll out the program.

'By that time, the learning is already overrun by the next learning. And you're always chasing something, so that actually you can never achieve the results that you desire. I think that's a big struggle. I think the big companies are entrapped.'

Baart's view is borne out by a quick look at the corporate successes of recent years. In the last decade we have seen emerging digital technologies transform analog businesses, from music and advertising to bricks-and-mortar stores, from hospitality, newspapers, and books to education and training. Leaders in traditional markets have been challenged and overtaken by digital-native or digital-born companies such as Amazon, Apple, Google, Spotify, Netflix, Airbnb, and others.

While last century was centered around manufacturing, finance, and the automotive industry, today the epicenter is technology and digital-native companies. They are creating new business models, reshaping the ways value is created, and rewriting what it means to be people-centric and technology savvy.

What's easy to see is that the new generation of leaders in charge of those businesses – Millennials and Generation Z, largely – are digital natives and they understand that technology may contribute towards disruption and change. They also recognize it will be an enabler to innovation and help them respond to the complex problems of the world. In other words, the emerging, exponential technologies can be the foundation on which to build new business models, new types of organization, and new operating models, among many other things.

They are bringing a new leadership mindset that says there has to be a better way to solve the big problems we are facing, a faster, more flexible, more adaptable way – a way of working that is more humane, inclusive, and innovative.

It's no surprise, then, to find next-generation leaders in an evolving conversation with employees, customers, partners, and communities about how organizations can generate transformative solutions through emerging technologies and their combined effects. They often see trends and innovation possibilities others don't. They are familiar with, and excited about, the social, educational, and business opportunities offered by the new technologies, the amount of data and connectivity. Arguably the most disruptive forces in the history of business are now being unleashed – 5G, mobile, cloud, robotics, artificial intelligence, machine learning, data analytics – and at an exponential pace. These technologies are revolutionizing industries and creating new sources of value for companies that know how to harness their power. They are not part of some futuristic concept anymore.

But it's not all down to technology. Traditional companies could have accessed the same technology as Amazon, now almost 50 years old with 500,000 employees; as Google, around 25 years old with 135,000 employees; and as Netflix, also around 25 years old, and growing on a daily basis. Success takes more than technology.

What makes digital native companies successful is their business model, fueled jointly by technology and an intense focus on engaging their employees, customers, and communities across different engagement mechanisms. They understand the power of communities, positive feedback loops, network effect, and having a clear purpose that motivates and inspires people who share the same vision.

They are clearly in tune with the fact that their success depends not only on technology but also on unleashing creativity by shifting power to people. They empower leaders, engineers, data scientists, and problem solvers at the edge of the business to harness the collective intelligence of communities and customers.

Many of these leaders understand that the path from idea to customer impact must take days not years. They have embraced inspiration, invention and impact powered by people to make it happen.

What I'm saying is there's a solid business case for learning new ways to innovate, create, and deliver value by harnessing the power and collective intelligence of people – employees, customers, partners, and communities. These digital native companies have redefined industry after industry, driving the global economy. And they are now redefining the science of management, strategy, execution, and organizational culture. They are leading, executing, and thinking differently.

For leaders in traditional companies the learning curve is greater. Besides the technical upskilling required, the need for a shift in mindset is even more urgent. A shift from efficiency, cost-cutting, and incremental changes to a more entrepreneurial mindset – a mindset of innovation fueled by people and technology, and experimentation with new ways of creating and delivering value to the customer. The customer experience – needs, concerns, inspirations, and feelings – should determine the technology and digitization choices, the skill development, and the value delivery partners, and not the other way around.

People-centered innovation, agility, decision-making, and execution require more connected, networked, and collaborative organizational models and cultures. Capacity for agility and resilience will be as much about distributed and networked teams, emergent communities of interest, and connecting people by shared meaning and purpose as it will be about acquiring and implementing the latest technologies.

So what can the new generation of leaders teach traditional companies about how to become people- and technology-centered innovators versus watching from the sidelines and imitating the winners? Because imitation is often a strategy that fails. Well, leaders in traditional companies must be willing to shift from protecting the *status quo* and ask themselves the following questions:

- How are their companies positioned for people-centered and collaborative innovation and value creation, not just technical?
- Are they willing to invest in innovation in novel ways?
- How can internal employees as well as external partners, customers, and communities become active agents of innovation for their business?

THE CONSTANT DANCE OF CHANGE

Banks Baker, Head of Global Partnerships at Google, gives the impression the whole organization is in constant motion and a dance of change.

'At Google, change is constant,' he says. 'The organizational structure changes at least every 18-24 months.' Probably faster.

'But there is no single way that Google manages internal change, like a reorganization. There is no change methodology that defines the change road map, how to get to the end-state most effectively. Because at Google, we often don't have a static end-state we're looking for; we need to maintain a fluidity in our structures to support the pace of our business.'

That's not to say that Google doesn't learn from the past.

'We continually study the older and more mature born-digital companies,' says Baker. 'Companies like Amazon, and Netflix, even Google, for their entrepreneurial and innovative approaches to customers, employees, agility and speed in product development and technology adoption.'

But it's never with a view to copying anything they see.

This way of working could hardly be more different from traditional organizations, built around a static, siloed, structural hierarchy.

It was Larry Page, Co-founder of Google, when he restructured Google's parent company as Alphabet in 2015[9], who captured this ethos well: 'We've long believed that over time companies tend to get comfortable doing the same thing, just making incremental changes. But in the technology industry, where revolutionary ideas drive the next big growth areas, you need to be a bit uncomfortable to stay relevant.' And I love that.

As a business change and transformation consultant, I have witnessed many traditional companies battle for survival in the face of relentless technology innovation, disruptive business models, and agile trailblazers taking their market share.

One of my clients, the Digital Transformation Executive in a *Fortune* 500 traditional company, shares with me his frustration at their inability to change and transform. 'We have not been successful in our attempts to transform digitally,' he says. 'We have long history of failed projects and investments.' He shakes his head, reflecting on the challenges.

'What we are doing now is to understand why this is happening and figure out what we need to do to change. We are bringing in a lot more talent from digital-native companies like Google, Facebook, and Amazon. We need to learn from them and adopt their mindset.'

A key aspect of the key digital mindset is agility. It's defined in the dictionary as 'the ability to move quickly and easily'. To be agile in business is therefore to be able to react quickly to the unexpected, to be able to adapt to a changing market environment, and to respond to consumer needs quickly.

In today's VUCA world, everyone needs to be able to move and change direction quickly and with ease. Agile organizations need people with an agile mindset – the mindset of change, adaptation, flexibility, and learning. Because it is the people with an agile mindset that give agile organizations powerful outcomes.

In traditional companies, agile transformations are blocked by hierarchies of authority, complex organizational structures, bureaucratic and restrictive processes, and command-and-control mindsets.

WHEN IT COMES TO AGILITY, SMALL IS BEAUTIFUL

Many modern companies like Google, as we've seen, and Huawei, the Chinese technology group, are structured in a radically different way from traditional organizations[10]. Huawei, for example, comprises small, specialist service teams that work on particular projects as needed. The group has fostered a culture that, rather than celebrating the past, focuses almost entirely on the need for change and improvement.

So it's clear – the successful born-digital companies are experimenting, adopting, and reiterating their organizations' operating models. Often, it has to be said, because they've never worked any other way.

'I recently hired a person to head the workplace experience team and his background is in innovation,' says Kim Bertz at Wells Fargo. 'He is bringing agile practices and principles into the organization. Rather than going behind the curtain for six months and then delivering, we are doing things faster, we're more iterative.'

Importantly, the success in agility hasn't come from just one individual, though, and neither has it come from adopting a radically different approach.

'The guy in workplace experience set up open brainstorming sessions where anyone can attend and there is no expectation [of a particular outcome]. He created a platform where you can have your voice and be heard. Everyone is welcome, both within the department and employees from other departments.'

All very normal you might think. But what about the outcome?

'He conducts these sessions maybe once a month. And a constant big outcome of the sessions is to show that sometimes the greatest ideas don't emerge from the top down. Another is that these brainstorming sessions spark new ideas and they connect ideas from different perspectives.'

Bertz is convinced that what might be seen as traditional workshop technologies can – when used well – generate powerful new lessons, innovative ideas, and build new engagement strongly across organizations.

Thomas Klein, People and Organization Leader at Jodel, a Berlin start-up focused on building local communities, is also passionate about building agile high-performing organizations and leadership teams. But he insists the aim is to remain human-centered.

'I don't know how it works in traditional companies since I never worked in one,' he says. 'However, in a start-up there is a big focus on the end-user, customer, and the market.' It's about the people, he says, and it's about keeping things real-time, in the here and now.

'There is a natural organizational agility where the team develop products and services to solve real-time customer challenges and there is a constant adjustment and reiteration. So consciously and continuously we check with the end-user and the market. Does it still solve the need or do we need to change something?'

This seems to solve most of the challenges facing Jodel as they occur. So much so that the idea of implementing a 'transformation program' seems illogical to him. 'Change and transformation, for example, it's not just a project,' he says. 'It's a continuous process of doing change every day of the week. You have to challenge your own assumptions and beliefs every day.'

SENSE AND RESPOND

Agility is also at the heart of how Cloudflare, a pioneering technology start-up in the US, operates, says Jayson Noland, Head of Investor Relations. The company, with its small teams, is quick to sense and respond. 'We launch products constantly, and it is never perfect. There are all sorts of bugs and errors.' There's a reason for this kind of launch. By the time it's perfect you've missed the market, he says.

'When we launch, the product is out there and we are learning and iterating. So we launch products, give it away free to customers, and they give us feedback. Then we iterate so fast to get the next version to the market.'

An agile leadership style was not a deliberate goal for Adrian Locher, a serial entrepreneur who founded his first internet company as he was graduating from university in Switzerland. It was all he could do when the 'fun side project' he had set up with a friend faced rapid and unexpected growth.

'I founded my first company in 2010 and sold it in 2015,' he explains. 'It started out as a side project with my co-founder while we were involved in many other projects, investments and other fancy things.' It was an e-commerce company, based on a mix of the Groupon model and the 'shopping club' model.

'We had never imagined the growth trajectory of the company when we started this venture. The company grew from zero to over $100m in revenue within five years and we went from zero employees to 180 within the first 12 months. We had $5m revenue in the first year and $30m in the second year. We were completely overwhelmed and surprised about this company taking off like crazy.'

He pauses, remembering the times.

'It was like a ride on a rocket that we could barely steer.'

Locher intuitively embraced a human-centric and agile leadership style to successfully grow the company at an accelerated pace. 'We had no idea how to manage the employees, high growth in revenue… we had no clue ourselves. We never imagined or planned for such an accelerated growth,' he says.

'So we just focused on the vision and goals and told people: now please find your way there and we will support you wherever we can. We saw our role as leaders to enable and empower our employees and the teams, setting the right direction and fertile ground where the business can grow.'

Locher epitomizes the entrepreneur with infectious passions, whether it's for people, AI technology, or the planet. He also instinctively trusts the people he works with – and that's just as well.

'We couldn't make every decision alone because we didn't know any better than our employees,' he says. 'We realized early in the process that we have to build a culture where we will hire extremely hungry and capable people who would go out and solve problems just in time versus report or create problems. Our approach was all about getting things done, empowering employees, celebrating successes along the way, and not micromanaging.' He's very clear on that point.

'We had to be very agile to keep up with the growth of the business. We didn't really have time to assess, analyze, and plan. Actually, we didn't even think in those terms, since I really didn't know how to even set up an agile organization. We didn't really know all the answers to that. We just started to lead from the front and be there for the employees and be the ones to take the first step.'

There was one step more than any other that made a difference, he says.

'I realized the importance of hiring the right people because that defines what your company will look like in the future. We also realized that, back in 2010 in Switzerland, it was hard to find talent with e-commerce skills and capabilities. E-commerce and internet were still in the early adoption stage and our first and most important problem was to find the right skills, the right people.'

What was the solution?

'We quickly realized that we will not find the right talent and we had to build it and develop our people on our own. We hired lots of young, bright, and hungry people and we developed them into becoming leaders themselves because we couldn't find those leaders out there.'

So here is a major lesson from next-generation leaders Kim Bertz, Thomas Klein, Jayson Noland and Adrian Locher, who provide insights into the leadership and organizational practices needed to build an agile culture:

- They put employees first and create an environment where employees can be empowered to make decisions, solve problems, and be part of building the business.

- They put customers at the center of product development, testing products with them, incorporating their feedback, and reiterating.

- A 'nothing is impossible' mindset. Employees at successful start-ups constantly optimize the way they work.
- A sense of purpose and belonging. This means making

sure that every employee knows that they can make a difference and that their work has a real impact on the company.

- An understanding of the importance of hiring the right talent and developing them and growing them with the business.

Perhaps these are strategies you're already using where you are, or perhaps you can adapt some of the ideas and make them relevant for your teams. The fact is that agile mindsets and practices are not developed on a moment's notice. You must continually reflect and ask the right questions to stay agile:

- Are you prioritizing customers over shareholders? An agile mindset believes if customers are happy and loyal, then shareholders are also happy.

- Do you operate with small, self-organizing and cross-functional teams or management-directed individuals?

- Do your communication and collaboration happen via networks or top-down hierarchies?

INNOVATION THROUGH TRANSPARENCY

Any type of transformation – agile, digital, people-centric, networked, open-innovation – in today's hyperconnected and interdependent world requires true transparency with everyone involved. Because transparency is one of the driving principles of an agile approach. So agile organizations strive to create transparency with customers, partners, and within their teams. Agile people practices like centrality of customer focus, iteration of small incremental releases, and receiving feedback from users after every release are all based on transparency. Of course, the principles of empathy and trust are an implied part of that, but let's focus on transparency for a moment.

As we saw earlier, transparency is at the heart of Cloudflare, a pioneering technology start-up in the US, says Jayson Noland, Head of Investor Relations. And while many companies find transparency a struggle, Cloudflare doesn't seem to. 'What we are doing is not rocket science,' Noland says. It is all about leading differently by establishing a culture of transparency.

'The culture of Cloudflare is so different. Everybody at the company has stand-up desks and nobody has a landline, nobody. The whole company can go see the CEO's calendar, it's incredibly transparent. Transparency to an extreme, I mean. There's not many companies out there where you could just go click a few times and see what the CEO's schedule is today or the CFO's schedule.'

Interestingly, the transparency within the company also extends outside, which he says leads to greater innovation. 'We launch new products all the time and the platform is open to external people. External people have the ability to build products on the Cloudflare platform. Anybody from anywhere in the world could write an application and drop into our platform and make it available in 200 cities around the world. Innovation is no longer kept in the walls of Cloudflare.'

This would not be possible in a traditional company, says Noland, who has extensive experience working with Silicon Valley giants such as HP, Cisco and Intel and many unicorn start-ups. 'That culture does not exist in traditional, large, and mature companies. All these new digital start-ups that are so successful, they should not exist. We should not exist.'

Noland has an interesting take on this.

'It should have been Cisco that built us. They have the technology, investment dollars, and know-how. Cisco can and does buy such start-ups but they can't retain the talent – the talent would leave.'

Transparency with the innovation it brings is simply not the culture of big companies, he says.

'You need to build such an innovative, start-up culture organically. I think large, traditional companies are inherently at a disadvantage when it comes to a culture of innovation and agile development – launch product to market, test with customers and stakeholders, reiterate.'[11]

Innovative companies today also tend to be part of larger innovation ecosystems. They create ecosystems where there is an exchange of technology, information, and experience among people, enterprises, start-ups, universities, governments, and research think-tanks. It is an open and collaborative innovation space. This is a significant shift from traditional hierarchical and control-based business operating models. In such companies, transparency in business is a taboo concept. The traditional models of success are based on the assumption that the more opaque your organization's operations are – the more you guard your company's secrets – the better your chances of success. That's according to the 'Knowledge is power' school of thought, anyhow.

But in today's hyperconnected digital economy, transparency is the gold standard.[12] Digital native companies are succeeding – both financially and in brand loyalty – by being radically open about the salaries of their leaders, for example, about the diversity of their workforce, and where and how they source materials. The new technologies are continually increasing customers' desire for transparency, authenticity, and ethical business practices.

A good example of this is the social media app maker Buffer, which is committed to building a cultural model for transparency in business.[13] When it decided to publish every single employee's salary on its website, applications soared and the quality of candidates improved, it says.

But transparency is a mindset as well as a business model. It can't just be this year's gimmick. Being transparent has to be part of the DNA of leaders and employees, at every level of the company, for it to take hold and create significant business value. Transparency also requires strong emotional intelligence from leaders. Because your failures are just as visible as your successes, maybe even more so.

Picking up on this issue of transparency, though, how transparent should a leader be? Rubin Lind, CEO and founder of a portfolio of companies including Skills4School in Germany, used to believe he should protect his team from the truth. But he now believes transparency is essential.

When an investor withdrew support, his company faced a financial crisis. 'How I handled this with the team really changed me as a leader,' he says. 'This was the first time I really had to think about the impact on the team and how I wanted to communicate the news to the team.'

He needed to find new investors, but this would take time. This meant he wouldn't be able to pay the team for a few months, but he didn't know how much to tell them. 'I struggled for weeks about what to do. I felt if I communicated the situation before I had secure funding, they might leave. If I told them about the financial crisis we were in, they might feel unsecure and leave anyway.'

It was a real quandary, he says.

He knew his team would feel powerless to fix the situation. 'They couldn't talk to investors or find funding. Because that was my job. I could just not offer them the security they needed.'

On the other hand, he says, he had a nagging feeling he should be transparent, especially if the plan didn't work. Shouldn't his team know, because it would impact their livelihoods? 'But I would rationalize and say, "I should keep this information to myself until I have the funding."'

Eventually the pressure overwhelmed him. 'I broke down and told them about the situation after a few weeks. I told them that I had made a mistake and kept a lot of information to myself. I told them I had the solution in my head, but I couldn't tell them. What if it didn't work?

'I also didn't want the pressure of everyone worrying and asking me how it was going. So I was really not transparent at all.'

When he told them, the team said they could see he was under a lot pressure. But by keeping the situation from them, he realized was 'not being a very nice guy', in his words.

'I thought I was being smart not telling them and focusing on the solution. But I learned it would have been smarter if I told them in the beginning. They would have felt more part of the team and part of the solution.'

It all worked out in the end. 'We got through it,' says Lind. 'We got the funding and grew the company. And in the process I also grew painfully and understood some lessons about leadership.'

The lessons for individuals seem clear then. But what exactly does an organization have to gain by opening itself up to scrutiny and competition? Does radical transparency contribute meaningfully to the success of a firm, or does a firm's success contribute to its radical transparency? What's the cause and what's the effect?

For me the question about radical transparency is inextricably linked to the question of how we might create a culture of people-centered innovation within our organizations. For many modern companies, both traditional and digital native, open innovation ecosystems comprising customers, partners, communities, and research institutions are a way of bringing innovative products to the market by tapping into the creativity and ideas of the people involved.

This type of people-centric innovation and harnessing the collective intelligence of communities requires radical transparency – opening up the company's internal knowledge, problems and challenges, technology and processes to the external partners, customers, and communities.

And that sparks other questions that may be useful for leaders to ask:

- How can we create a culture of creativity, innovation, and execution rather than a culture just driving towards efficiency?

- How can we create an entrepreneurial mindset and adopt new technologies or business models that will anticipate and meet our customers' unstated or future needs?

- How do we rebuild our company and our culture for continuous innovation and never be satisfied with *status quo*?

You'll notice 'innovation' is a key word in a couple of these questions. Because an agile mindset and innovation go hand in hand. In agile organizations that value transparency, collaboration, and continuous change, people are empowered to have more ideas, they are empowered to share them, and they practice an approach you could describe as 'experiment, test, and reiterate'.

Successful agile companies empower people to collaborate in self-organizing, diverse teams and challenge the *status quo* and industry best practices. And when teams are empowered, the more likely they are to experiment, to learn, to improve performance, to innovate, and to increase the competitive advantage and generate growth.

Companies can approach their journey to agility and innovation from many different starting points. In my view, the secret behind agile and innovative companies is that they start from a people-centric perspective. They are customer-obsessed. They tap into their employees' ideas and let them experiment and create as many channels as possible for communicating, sharing, and building on those ideas.

They create a culture of innovation where there are many channels for expression, recognizing that different people and different ideas will percolate up in different ways. They allow downtime during daily business to take a step back and think or reflect on their ideas and areas they are passionate about.

Unstructured time can positively affect the creativity and empowerment of employees. For example, 3M of the US pursues a well known 15 per cent strategy where everyone is allowed to devote about 15 per cent of their time to 'experimental doodling'.[14] Google has a similar rule, where engineers can devote 20 per cent of their time to their own initiatives. Moreover, Google also has what it calls FixIts, 24-hour sprints where Google staff, known of course as Googlers, drop everything and focus 100 per cent of their energy on solving a specific problem.

If you enable employees to pursue projects they care deeply about, innovation can follow. For example, Facebook's Celebrate Pride, a tool that helps users show support for the LGBTQ community by adding a rainbow filter to their profile picture, was built by two interns during a Facebook hackathon. It was inspired by a flag waving on Facebook's Menlo Park campus in June, Gay Pride month, and the team made the tool ready for global launch in just 72 hours.

The outcome? Over one weekend, more than 26m people updated their profile pictures with the tool. And there were more than 500m interactions with these photos during the weekend when the US Supreme Court was reaching a decision on marriage equality.

So any company can benefit from learning how to better attract and manage innovators, foster engagement, and ultimately lead to success: by thinking in small, diverse, empowered teams.

In traditional companies things are quite different. I have observed a cultural mindset there that assumes the more complex the problems are, the more brainpower is required to solve them. This results in more and more people being included in a program who don't really need to be there and who don't contribute much value. I have been in programs where 20-30 team members needed to be aligned, co-coordinated, and informed to move things forward.

The result? Everything is slow – communication, alignment, and decision-making. And sadly the focus on the customer is non-existent thanks to the complex internal processes.

Agile and innovative organizations, on the other hand, are made up of small, empowered teams with a compelling purpose. And they can solve the challenges that really matter to the business, customers, and stakeholders.

'You don't really know what value these little teams can create,' says Noland from Cloudflare. 'It could be huge. And if it fails, it doesn't make a huge loss for the company.'

So, in a nutshell, what's the benefit of leading small teams?

'With a bunch of small teams,' he says, 'you end up with lots of innovative ideas and leadership opportunities for young people. There is less of an emphasis on degrees and backgrounds in start-ups – some of the most famous founders in the world didn't finish college.'

In more traditional companies, though?

'In more mature companies, there is a fear of failing that keeps people with creative ideas hostage. They don't launch a product or idea until they feel it's just perfect.' So stay small is the best advice.

Keeping teams small is not the only key to managing exponential change. There's something even more critical: you need as many viewpoints within those teams as possible. The only question is, how? How do you bring in such diverse viewpoints and how do you manage radically diverse teams? ■

“People ask me all the time how we have been able to recruit and retain so many talented investors that happen to be women. It’s really not that complicated. Women want to work somewhere where they see other incredibly talented women in seats of authority, influence, and risk-taking. And the really great news is that once you reach a critical mass, you actually don’t have to talk about it that much anymore. The diverse talent actually comes and finds you.

Katie Koch
Co-Head, Fundamental Equity
Goldman Sachs Asset Management

Chapter 3

DIVERSITY AND INCLUSION: THE SECRET SAUCE OF INNOVATION

Toward the human experience

I believe diversity is a fundamental attribute of successful teams and I'll explain why. First of all, let's look at innovation, which depends on new ideas. And people from diverse backgrounds, with different perspectives and experiences, certainly do bring new and interesting ideas.

Not only does innovation emerge from new ideas, though. Innovation happens when diverse teams challenge the *status quo*, looking beyond the obvious, to bring in different perspectives and to work creatively together. If everyone on the team had a similar world view, went to the same school or received a similar education, they would all reach the same conclusions. When you have a diverse and inclusive workplace, however, you can unleash an explosion of ideas and innovations in your organization.

So that's why innovative organizations need diversity and inclusion – in order to innovate. And to survive today, innovation is a must.

Innovative organizations know that fostering diversity and inclusion – the extent to which the leaders as well as teams throughout the organization are diverse across age, gender, ethnicity, industry, sexual orientation, and cultural backgrounds – is critical. The most inclusive, equal, and diverse workplace cultures are 11 times more innovative, according to research by Accenture.[15]

How do you foster diversity and inclusion? Well, to foster diversity of ideas, perspectives, and experiences, leaders must see, listen to, and empathize with their employees, customers, and partners. Leaders must be good at inclusion, through soliciting and amplifying other people's voices. When you invite each member of your team into a discussion by name, you are demonstrating that you see them and hear them, and by implementing their unique ideas and solutions you help them become as equally invested and committed as you are to the success of the project.

Katie Koch at Goldman Sachs Asset Management (GSAM) oversees about $60bn in assets globally, which she describes as '60bn little equity businesses'. Unusually, about half of the portfolio managers in her team are women, well above industry average. But for Koch, improving all types of diversity is not simply the right thing to do – it is a business imperative.

'Diversity is at the core of what we do,' she says. 'I'm in the business of fundamental equity investing, which is human-driven investing. And what we're trying to do every day is create an edge by having a unique perspective relative to the market. And one of the ways to cultivate that perspective is by bringing in people with different views and backgrounds. Ensuring there is a diverse set of voices at the table so that our collective understanding is less naïve and less biased.'

HOW DO YOU BUILD A DIVERSE TEAM?

It's one thing saying you want a diverse team, but it's another thing actually building one.

'People ask me all the time how I have been able to recruit and retain so many talented investors that happen to be women,' says Koch.

'It's really not that complicated. Women want to work somewhere where they see other incredibly talented women in seats of authority, influence, and risk-taking. That's the best evidence that the organization does, in fact, value diverse perspectives, and that they will be able to move forward with their career.'

A strong commitment to create a diverse and inclusive organization can become a 'virtuous cycle', referring to events that reinforce one another through a continuous positive feedback loop.

'The really great news is that, once you reach a critical mass, which we've been able to do on gender, you actually don't have to talk about it that much anymore and obsess over it. The diverse talent actually comes and finds you. And that's just a really great place to be.'

Koch gives an example of what she means. 'If we think about the cultural lens for a second, the head of our global equity team is an incredibly talented investor named Alexis Deladerrière. Unlike most people at Goldman Sachs in New York, Alexis actually grew up on a farm in the south of France. And after 15 years of working in London, we relocated him to New York and he brought a lot of European experience and perspective to running our global effort. While we've been, for example, integrating environmental, social and governance factors (ESG) into our process for 10 years, the focus on ESG-related issues was much more pronounced in Europe. His experience in this area has really helped us take our approach to the next level.'

So what did he do for Goldman Sachs?

'He heightened our awareness around the dramatic transition to a low carbon economy,' she says. He told them they were on the cusp of a sustainable investing revolution, adding, 'It's going to have the scale of the industrial revolution and the speed of the digital revolution.'

Such transatlantic insights helped the team change its strategy. 'His perspectives really added to our confidence to reduce traditional carbon-based assets across our portfolios,' says Koch, 'at the same time as leaning into solution providers to key environmental issues. That's been really helpful to performance and we got there because of his diverse perspective.'

She also values working with people of different ages. 'Another example of unique perspectives would be the importance of bringing in viewpoints from different generations,' she says. 'One of our portfolio managers is an exceptionally talented woman named Laura Destribats. She's a really great investor and also a young Millennial. Laura attuned us to the incredible opportunity at the intersection of consumer and technology. And some of the Generation X and Baby Boomers on our team were really skeptical about Millennials. You know, "Aren't those the kids still living in my basement? Do they really have any money to spend? Why are we focused on their tastes and preferences?"' And she laughs.

'But Laura was quick to point out that Millennials were the world's largest demographic cohort with 2.3bn people. Their spending was set to increase over the next five years by 17 per cent. Whereas Baby Boomers' spending was likely to shrink by 10 per cent.

'And therefore, with her perspectives, we were early to understand the dynamics of tech-enabled consumption, from e-commerce to movie streaming, and Millennial preferences for experiences, healthy lifestyle, and their commitment to sustainability. We were able to understand all of that well ahead of the market, which, again, has been really beneficial to performance.'

Koch, for one, understands that Millennials are demanding that organizations value and be intentional about diversity and inclusion. They understand that to harness the power of rapidly emerging new technologies requires building diverse and inclusive teams that reflect the mindsets and backgrounds of the end customer while bringing a variety of experiences and worldviews to the table.

Diversity alone, though, isn't enough. It's also about including everyone's thoughts and experiences in the day-to-day of the business and valuing their thoughts and experience. Inclusivity is the twin sister of diversity. As Vernā Myers, thought leader in cultural change, puts it, 'Diversity is being invited to the party. Inclusion is being asked to dance.' Diversity doesn't stick, she says, without inclusion being part of the mix.[16]

There is a wealth of evidence that companies with great diversity outperform their peers by a significant margin, and it has become a business imperative. Yet progress in corporations is slow. According to the 2021 Women in the Workplace report by McKinsey, in American corporations only 24 per cent of C-Suites are made up of women and only 4 per cent are women of color.[17]

However, the next generation of leaders don't like to debate diversity quotas or the potential return on investment of diversity. They instinctively understand diversity and inclusion are important conditions for better innovation, creativity, and performance.

This generation, however, is not being passive. Many new leaders are actively pushing back when they hear excuses like, 'We are not able to find the right candidate.'

Anne-Sophie d'Andlau, Co-founder of CIAM asset management, with bases in Paris and London, hears this particular excuse all the time.

'In the hedge fund world,' she says, 'being a woman was an uphill battle most of the time. Most of the time I didn't feel I was part of the team or culture.' So she just focused on doing her job, working super-hard. But feeling very unwelcome.

'Basically, France is not known to be super-welcoming for woman, especially in the finance and investment industry. Even though women work a lot, compared to other countries.' It's still a fight, she says.

'Just a year ago, we were recruiting for an open leadership position, and I was really pushing to hire a woman.'

How did it work out?

'After some time my COO tells me, "I can't find any woman candidates. Out of 30 résumés, I received only two. Don't ask me to find a woman, it's difficult."'

D'Andlau was exasperated.

'I told him to go back. It's less easy to find a woman because they're not going to just go on your plate, like right away. Maybe they don't sell themselves as well as men, but go back. I'm sure there's one out there that is going to be like the perfect person for the situation.'

What happened?

'He found her and she's here.'

So the new generation of leaders are not willing to accept that argument of 'lack of qualified women applicants'. They are digging deeper and asking, 'Why are we not able to find women applicants? Are we looking in the right places? Are we too quick to qualify out women applicants?'

Goldman Sachs Asset Management is one company focused on promoting board diversity at its portfolio companies through its engagement efforts and proxy voting. In 2019, it voted against directors of 250 companies in the US because of their lack of gender diversity.

'The best way to drive change is to engage with companies to raise key issues like diversity while concurrently using your vote to reinforce this message. You don't want to be antagonistic – you need to be willing to vote against managements where necessary – but you also need to try to be part of the solution,' says Katie Koch.

'And so one of the great parts about Goldman Sachs is that we have this incredible network. We engaged with these companies, told them what our intentions were on voting, and when they expressed interest in bringing a woman on board but highlighted that they didn't know the right woman, we provided many of them with lists of qualified women to help in that process.'

About 67 per cent of those companies Koch refers to have since added at least one woman to the board.

'After having had success in the US, it built our confidence to take that policy global,' she says. The following year, Goldman Sachs Asset Management voted against 1,719 directors at 898 companies, not just in the US but worldwide.

Koch is laser focused on this. If Goldman Sachs Asset Management is diverse, and the companies it invests in are diverse, it's better for everyone.

'Diversity of perspectives can help drive better performance in our portfolios, helping us consider new ways of driving innovation and transformation,' she says.

There's another area of diversity that is less often discussed. You don't simply need people from a variety of backgrounds, you also need people whose brains are wired in different ways. This is known as cognitive diversity and the theory of multiple intelligences.

US psychologist Howard Gardner, for example, has identified nine different intelligences (*Multiple Intelligences*, 2006):

1. naturalist,
2. musical,
3. logical-mathematical,
4. existential,
5. interpersonal,
6. bodily-kinesthetic,
7. linguistic,
8. intra-personal,
9. and spatial.

There's more on cognitive bias in the brilliant *Thinking Fast and Slow* (2011). Nobel Prize winner Daniel Kahneman relates the story of his work with Amos Tversky on two ways of seeing the world – one system is fast, intuitive and emotional. The other is slow, logical and deliberative. Both matter.

But no matter whose work you look at, it's clear. Ensuring a diversity of thinking and a balanced mixture of intelligences and experiences on a leadership team or board is not just important – it's mission critical. Because you must ensure risks, threats, opportunities, and even daily events are examined in multidimensional ways. So diversity and inclusion in its many forms could provide the richness and holistic insight you and your business need for far better decision-making, innovation, and execution.

No matter how important the era of exponential technologies is for the future success of companies, it is the people not technology that is driving the Fourth Industrial Revolution.

I call this the Human Experience or HX revolution.

WELCOME TO THE HX REVOLUTION

Early in my career, one of the most valuable books I came across was John Naisbitt's *Megatrends: Ten New Directions Transforming Our Lives* and I was captivated by one quote in particular. 'The greatest breakthroughs of the 21st century won't occur because of technology,' he said. 'They will occur because of an expanding concept of what it means to be human.'

The book was originally published in 1982, but I believe that it's only now that we are entering an era of human-centered organizations and people-centered leadership. And people-centered leaders do just one thing: put people first.

Making human experience the core focus means genuinely caring about people. It means embracing humanistic values, such as empathy, authenticity, vulnerability, interconnectedness, and respect.

Klaus Schwab, the German economist and Founder of the World Economic Forum, links the need to put people first with the digital disruption caused by the Fourth Industrial Revolution.

'Let us together shape a future that works for all by putting people first,' he says, 'empowering them and constantly reminding ourselves that all of these new technologies are first and foremost tools made by people for people.' (Learn more in Schwab's 2016 manifesto.)

I'm not sure that digital disruption is the sole reason we should be doing this, but I'm sure that the key differentiator for companies is now the Human Experience – the experience businesses create for employees, customers, partners, and stakeholders. It's an experience that puts people – traditionally at the endpoint of a transaction – first and at the center. But it's not as easy as it sounds, especially if you want it not to sound like a cliché.

'For me, leadership comes down to the ability to put people first and listen,' says Paulo Pontin, the Managing Partner responsible for Verizon telecommunications group in Latin America. 'You've got to build empathy for the people that you're entrusted to serve – your team, employees, customers, partners, so on.'

How do you do that in practice?

'Your ability to listen and have empathy are related to your Emotional Intelligence,' he says, that is, your ability to read what other people as well as you yourself are feeling. 'And emotional intelligence is really relevant in the current business environment of so much uncertainty and change.'

In his leadership role, Pontin focuses on national and international business development, connecting companies, executives, and communities. He is a mentor for start-ups – at the invitation of São Paulo City Hall – as well as other corporations, incubators, and accelerators.

Why Pontin's experience is worth listening to is that he is working in an environment that is in constant change due to the rapid technology innovations and digital transformation that is impacting his industry.

For the last decade, he has learned that the leadership challenge of the 21st century is not technology, but leading people with a humanistic approach. Putting people first. He has focused on developing his people-centric skills and believes, given the rapid rate of change, the people element is far more central to his leadership and organization's success.

'For example,' he says, 'we are now accelerating digital transformation and a lot of people are afraid of losing their jobs to bots, robots or machines.' In addition, there are lots of fears around pandemics and what's still to come.

'How many ways shall we face the future? I try to coach my team to live in the present but with an eye on the future, because it is important to live in the present and know what is going on now.'

Pontin himself makes sure he lives in the present, in his personal life as well as his professional role. He is passionate about music – playing guitar, bass, keyboard, and harmonica – and is a member of two bands. And in spite of his busy schedule, he always saves time for his family and meditation practice.

It's important for a leader to know his or her team members well, he says. 'As leaders you have to have emotional intelligence to engage and understand how your employees are doing, personally and professionally. How are they dealing with their fears and uncertainties about the future? How can I promote the sense of belonging or how can I restore that belonging if they have lost it somehow?'

He believes that the idea of people-centric leadership is becoming the new normal. And it's not just him. There is a campaign in his company, from the CEO down, to pay more attention to colleagues as people first.

'I think concepts like emotional intelligence, empathy, and transparency are becoming more part of the new normal with the new generation of leaders,' he says. They are changing the way people relate to each other.

PSYCHOLOGY AND BELIEFS AREN'T GLOBAL

Global corporate psychology, belief, and behaviors are not universal – they are strongly influenced by Western culture. As described earlier, the industrial movements and their theories about capitalism, machine-like organizations, and management theories were developed largely in North America and Europe. However, these paradigms, beliefs and behaviors were exported to many other cultures as the globalization of capitalism grew. When I refer to 'people-centered practices', it is important to acknowledge this pro-Western bias and respect the fact that people's self-identity, values, and behaviors are also shaped by the culture they live in.

Pontin acknowledges the cultural differences. Latin American cultures tend to be interdependent and relationship focused in comparison with other Western cultures.

'We in Latin America are much more used to having a more personal and people-centered approach even at work.' And he gives an example.

'The company just implemented a meeting practice – once again this is quite normal for Latin Americans. We now have a new meeting protocol – before we go into the agenda, we take the first five to 10 minutes to go around the table and do a professional and personal check-in with each other. It is an open discussion. You can talk about what is going on with your family or hobbies or something you achieved at work.'

What's this for?

'The purpose behind this practice is about creating a more personal connection and building better relationships. When you jump straight into the agenda, it is so cold and impersonal. I noticed that, as we feel more comfortable with this type of icebreaker, people are more proactively participating and sharing during the meeting. So it works.'

Such behavior would not be remarkable outside the office, he says. 'That human connection – at one point we lost it in corporations. As humans, we do this naturally – check in with each other and do some small talk before jumping into business topics. Because we are humans and we are interested in each other.'

But at some point we stopped. 'We lost that connection to our humanity,' he says. 'We became very mechanistic and focused on quarterly results, KPIs, numbers – not on people.'

So as the new generation of leaders begin to take up leadership roles across organizations, gear up for another paradigm shift – toward a people-centric leadership style.

While machines might be set to take over many technical tasks, people are very much at the heart of the future of work. Research on the future of work increasingly places high premiums on uniquely human skills.[18] The result of this will likely be more creative, human-centered jobs, requiring higher degrees of social and emotional intelligence, and negotiation skills.

So far we have made a lot progress focusing on customer experience (CX). It is the elusive differentiator every business is chasing. However, focusing on only one dimension of human experience is limiting in couple of ways. First, people are much more than customers or end users. They are humans with aspirations, fears, needs, emotions, and a constant need for meaning and relationships. To put them in a box as a customer limits their experience and our potential relationship with them. Second, businesses are social enterprises, and success depends on interconnections, interdependencies, and collaboration between many people. To successfully deliver customer experience requires many people to work together and the experiences of each of them matter.

So the human experience revolution (HX) expands the scope of experiences that make a business successful or not – in many dimensions.

Between the company and customers. Between colleagues. Between the company and suppliers. Between leaders, managers, and employees. Between company and communities.

And what's clear to me, exploring the accelerating acceptance of diversity and inclusion in the business world, is that the next generation of leaders – the New Leaders of Change I'm focusing on in this book – demonstrate exactly the qualities for humanistic, people-centered leadership that we need. They have strong concern for human and environmental wellbeing, for diversity and leading with purpose, for values and

Table 3: The human experience manifesto

1. **THE PARAMOUNT ELEMENTS:** A recognition that authenticity, trust, diversity, inclusion, and respect are paramount to being an effective leader.

2. **WE ARE WHOLE HUMAN BEINGS:** A sense that employees, partners, and customers are whole human beings. And that we all have similar struggles, emotions, aspirations, and disappointments.

3. **COMPASSION AND EMPATHY:** A belief that leaders should be compassionate and able to demonstrate empathy. It is a fallacy to think human beings can separate their work and life identities and create some kind of balance. People are not 'the workforce', 'human resources', 'head count' or 'human capital'. Such concepts should be consigned to the factory system of the 19th and 20th centuries.

4. **ENABLERS NOT SUPERIORS:** Leaders should be enablers of employee creativity and innovation versus power holders, decision-makers or seeing themselves as superior in any way. All employees are equal and make valuable contributions.

5. **VALUING INTERCONNECTIONS:** That leaders should value service to others and the interconnection of all living beings and the environment. Making the world a better place means making it better for all living things that inhabit the world and the environment. Making a living and making the world a better place are not mutually exclusive.

6. **AWARENESS AND MEANING-MAKING:** Leaders should also understand the deeper human need for self-awareness, finding meaning, and having a greater purpose in one's life.

emotional intelligence.

If I had to boil it down, I'd say the humanistic manifesto has the principles laid out in Table 3. And I know some will say that some or all of these are obvious. So why write it down when it seems so clear?

Well, so far, a 20th century mindset continues to operate across the majority of the business world. And that seems to amplify the common challenges we face instead of solving them. Claus Dierksmeier, Chair of Globalization Ethics at the University of Tübingen in Germany, and a board member for an international think-tank, the Humanistic Management Network, puts it like this: 'Many of the multiple crises human kind faces at the dawn of the 21st century share a common denominator: an economic system with only marginal regard for human values and virtues.'[19]

So perhaps this is why I feel it's necessary to craft a manifesto for people-centered leadership, elevating the experiences of people, all living things, and the planet above quarterly financial results and creating value for shareholders as the singular goal of business.

Or perhaps because, without its people, an organization is nothing, as Venetia Bell, Head of Strategy at GIB Asset Management, says. 'The core principle of my leadership and change management is quite a people-centric approach. I think it comes from the fact that organizations are not really a thing that exists. That it's not really a thing that you can point to and say, "here is a cup". It's always going to be quite a hard thing to pin it down.'

She pauses to gather her thoughts.

'Organizations ultimately exist because they are a collection of people who come together, who want to achieve something together, work collectively, and you kind of put a name and a brand around it to try and make that a bit of a clearer definition, but ultimately, it's just a concept.' She shrugs.

'I certainly subscribe to the school of thought that organizations do better when they are able to find a way to get that sense of belonging and identity as fundamental human beings. I think you get that collective identity by speaking to people's hearts and minds and seeing them as whole beings and setting up a really exciting vision and purpose that we can achieve together, and doing the things that will ultimately make a difference.'

Another reason I myself feel the need to craft a manifesto for the human experience revolution is that some of the next generation of leaders I've been talking with have learned the importance of human-centered leadership through negative experience.

'After my MBA, I joined a real estate finance firm in NY and underwrote very large real estate deals,' says Tara Hovey, now President and Chief Operating Officer at Optima, the family real estate business. 'Some of my best learning was actually the aspects I didn't like about the job and the company. Even though I was in a leadership position, I felt like I was a cog-in-the-wheel, where I was not able to see the big picture.'

And she wondered: 'Where was this business going? What was the meaning behind all this? Where do I fit in? It didn't feel meaningful to me.'

This experience was useful for her when she returned to her family's business in Chicago, where she had worked in all aspects of the business as a teenager before she did her MBA.

'I WAS KEENLY AWARE OF THE HUMAN SIDE'

'When I went back to our family business as a leader, I was so keenly aware of the human side of the business,' Hovey says. And she was inspired: how could she make sure everyone in the business knew how important their role was and how they served a purpose?

'After my MBA and working in NY and coming back to the family business, everything was about people. I wanted to create an environment and culture where everybody felt like they belonged, where everybody felt empowered to raise their hand with some crazy idea to throw out there, where people felt heard and respected.'

So she spent a lot of time getting to know people.

'I either had one-on-one lunches or would go for a walk around the block. I wanted to know what was working, what wasn't working, what motivated them. I just wanted to get a really good idea of their experience in the firm.'

Some people might wonder – did taking so much time simply to listen to employees actually help much? She's sure it did.

'Taking that time allowed me to lead much more effectively and make the needed changes. And there was so much change that happened in the next few years.'

This strategy works for Hovey, because there is no simpler way to exhibit human-centric leadership than to cultivate a sense of belonging in employees. When people have a sense of belonging, they feel listened to, accepted, respected, and free from judgment. Belonging also bolsters resilience and reduces stress. While individual employees can help others feel like they belong, a culture of belonging comes in large part from leaders – as demonstrated by both Venetia Bell and Tara Hovey.

Beyond creating this sense of belonging, the human-centered organization is one that exists to fulfill a meaningful purpose for its employees, customers, and community. Because this is the ultimate human experience, isn't it – to live our lives with purpose and meaning? In fact, fostering meaning and purpose may be the best-kept secret to building thriving businesses and careers.

We don't wake up in the morning as model customers, employees, leaders, or partners. We don't sit at our favorite restaurant and take the first bite of our favorite meal with the perfect sip of wine and think, 'I am the customer of this restaurant and end-user of this perfect meal.' So why do we insist on placing people in groups and objectifying them with abstract labels? We are human. We are complex, inconsistent, and most of all, emotional. It is time for businesses to acknowledge and respect that, and bring the human into focus.

So I believe, to succeed in the 21st century, where the power and reach of digital technologies are growing exponentially and the use of AI and augmented intelligence is rising, we need to re-establish and reconnect with our own humanity and the humanity of others. We need urgently to articulate what defines us as human and what it means to create experiences that are human.

We need to create a sense of belonging and purpose. And the next generation of leaders is showing us the way.

But who are these New Leaders of Change exactly? And what do they bring to the modern corporation, in practical terms? ■

"What I learned as a leader working with the older generation, 45-50 years old, is to be vulnerable and open to feedback. When we have a disagreement, I say, "This has worked for me in my career so far and I believe in this way. However, prove me wrong, you are the one with more experience." It is easier to build trust then and to discuss issues in an objective way.

Jonas Muff
CEO
Vara

Chapter 4

THE NEW WORLD OF INTERGENERATIONAL LEADERSHIP

Building people-centered communities

It snowballed quickly. 'I started building a community of people working together on addressing the energy transition mostly by having lots of conversations, giving talks at conferences, and reaching out to people.'

Andrea Ruotolo is speaking of her time setting up a community of innovators and disrupters while she was Global Head, Distributed Energy Systems, for Worley, the engineering group.

As an example of a leader working in a people-centric way, you can't get better than this.

'My intuition told me I had to connect with people at all levels of the organization, not only the people working at my level and those in upper management,' she says. 'I had lots of conversations with front-line employees to better understand what they thought about various issues, and what they were seeing from where they stand. What problems do they see? What do they want to change? How do they feel about the changes taking place in our industry? What is their energy level about these issues? Do they have potential? What ideas would they propose for how we can do things better as a company?'

Ruotolo wasn't very concerned about where they were in the organization today. She wanted to understand their level of motivation to grow and adapt with the changes that are happening in the energy sector. And, if so, what resources and support would they need to advance more quickly than they had done so far?

'The changes in the energy sector are so complex and demanding, I knew we would not be able to evolve fast enough if our people were not fully bought in and aligned to learning and working in new ways. So I spent quite a lot of time getting to know people at the human level. I started working with them on their overall career development, mentoring my younger team members not only on the technical content, but also at the human level, on how they saw themselves today and who they wanted to grow into being. So the community of people working to accelerate the energy transition started growing organically, because people were excited to be part of what we were working on, not only because those higher up in the company were calling for it, but because being involved was something to aspire to.'

The way Ruotolo worked with the company's leaders to set the strategic direction, but also went straight to the employees to connect with them at the human level and to get their input and engagement in the process, is typical of the way the new generation of leaders work. And it's important to recognize this, as the change in the workplace demographics is adding layers of complexity to organizations. No matter which generation we belong to, we must be equipped to mobilize and inspire an intergenerational workforce.

But let's step back a second. Because for the first time in history, there are five generations in the workplace[20]:

- Traditionalists – born 1925 to 1945
- Baby Boomers – born 1946 to 1964
- Generation X – born 1965 to 1980
- Millennials or Generation Y – born 1981 to 2000
- Generation Z – born 2001 to 2020

While there is often debate around exactly which years we're talking about here, these broad generations or cohorts of people share historical, political, societal, and economic experiences, that's certain. And the assumption of governments, policy makers, and marketers, among others, is that shared experiences at similar ages create similarities among people. First of all, in terms of personal attributes, attitudes, motivations, personalities, and political orientations. But also in their attitudes and behaviors related to work. Of course, these generational differences will also vary by gender, culture, country, and socioeconomic status.

But there's an important caveat. Because I wouldn't suggest making any assumptions about an individual based on their membership of any generational cohort. We are all individuals and see the world our own way.

However, an understanding of common generational differences may be useful, particularly when the age gap between an employee and a manager is significant.

REVISITING MULTIGENERATIONAL DIVERSITY

Before we can do that, we need to revisit the issue of age-based or multigenerational diversity. Because a spread of ages within a team leads to a wide range of ideas and knowledge, boosting cognitive diversity, and giving a company a competitive edge – counter-intuitively – by accelerating the change process.[21]

And in a world of fast-paced change, accelerating the change process can be a significant competitive advantage, as we've seen. In other words, inclusive decision-making, both ways between generations, can contribute directly to the bottom line.

Chip Conley, the US entrepreneur, strategist, author, and founder of the Modern Elder Academy, puts it like this: 'I believe, looking at the modern workplace, that the trade agreement of our time is opening up these intergenerational pipelines of wisdom so that we can all learn from each other.'[22]

Generations can successfully work with each other in a number of ways, he says. What Conley calls reverse mentoring is an inverted relationship where a younger employee coaches a more experienced employee to acquire knowledge or skills. Reciprocal mentoring, on the other hand, is when the older and younger generations learn from each other and discover new ways to connect, communicate, and engage.

When Conley joined Airbnb, the vacation rentals platform, as Head of Global Hospitality and Strategy, he found he was twice the age of his colleagues. Virtually a company elder, he found himself bringing not only his extensive hospitality expertise, but decades of emotional intelligence to the technology start-up. He knew how to get things done by building rapport, trust, and engagement, rather than grabbing power.

In a short time, many young Airbnb employees sought him out for mentoring and advice, appreciating his non-technical leadership experience and wisdom.

But he also learned a great deal about technology working with Airbnb employees. He may have had the Emotional Intelligence, but they had what he calls Digital Intelligence in spades.

It's this mutually valuable exchange of experience that helped him see modern elders are as much interns as mentors, because their 'beginner's mind and catalytic curiosity is a life-affirming elixir… for everyone'.

Reverse and reciprocal mentoring models are still relatively new in corporations, but are very relevant for companies with a multigenerational workforce. And Conley urges all organizations to capitalize on the alchemy, as he calls it, between older workers' wisdom and younger workers' technical skills.

Someone who's negotiated the generations in his short leadership career is Jonas Muff. He's not yet 30 years old, but is the CEO and Founder of Vara, a Berlin-based technology company that builds AI solutions for medical imaging. Before Vara he was the CEO of MX Healthcare, a cloud diagnostic platform heavily augmented by machine learning for medical specialists.

Both Vara and MX Healthcare are spin-offs from Merantix, the AI venture studio, whose founders, Rasmus Rothe and Adrian Locher, both value the know-how that older generations bring. Why? They ensure start-ups successfully advance from idea to launch to scale, creating revenue and profitability in the earliest days. So they deliberately recruit older people to work side-by-side with young entrepreneurs like Muff, who's learned a great deal from the experience.

'What I learned as a leader working with the older generation, 45-50 years old, is to be vulnerable and open to feedback,' says Muff. 'When we have a disagreement, I say, "This has worked for me in my career so far and I believe in this way. However, prove me wrong, you are the one with more experience." It is easier to build trust then and to discuss issues in an objective way.'

What has Muff found the most important aspect of intergenerational leadership?

'Showing vulnerability is super-important to me as a founder. And always remember why you hired people. Keep reminding yourself that they are here to help you and you brought them here because they are very good at something, but you are still in charge because you are the founder and you see the bigger picture. This approach has worked for me very well.'

OLDER PEOPLE – HOWEVER YOU DEFINE OLD – CAN BENEFIT A YOUNG COMPANY

So Muff strongly believes that older people – however you define old – can benefit a young company. 'People who are 45, 50, 60 have more experience and they are just wiser than you are,' he says. 'They have been shaped by life and it has shaped their character and their personality. They are in your team so you can learn from them and, in difficult situations, these people make a difference in your company.'

Without that experience, young founders of start-ups may cause chaos and disruption by trying to scale up their companies without the right structures and processes in place. Felicia Würtenberger, CHRO, or rather Humans, Vibes and Structures at Flooz in Germany, has first-hand experience of this through working as an HR consultant with start-up founders.

'As we were scaling up,' she says of one start-up, 'we hired a lot of senior people with a lot of experience, so they then recruited their own teams and built up their organization.'

How did that work out?

'The young founders and very young teams found that the experienced senior leaders brought much more focus, good prioritization, some key process and communication structures that helped deal with chaos and brought some calm.'

Sometimes younger leaders, who value a more human-centric way of working, think they don't need the structures and processes espoused by older generations. But Würtenberger believes the two things are not mutually exclusive. 'In my opinion we, the younger generations, still need structure and processes,' she says, 'and we need people who are in charge and owning things and driving things forward.'

What don't they want?

'What we don't want is this atmosphere of competition and fear, hierarchy, and ego and power. That's what we don't need anymore. And

I think you can have a structure and ownership and responsibilities also with a very emotional, intelligent, and human atmosphere.'

Clearly, a start-up has to be innovative, testing ideas that have not been tested before, but they must also have the potential to grow. And to grow and scale exponentially, start-ups need a range of processes. They need to ensure they are hiring the right talent, have the right organizational structure, have repeatable processes, have robust financial transparency and so on. This is where the know-how of older generations can be a critical success factor.

MANAGING MANY PERSPECTIVES IS A CHALLENGE

Managing a multi-generational workforce with so many different perspectives, experiences, values, and goals poses a unique challenge for next-generation managers and leaders. However, generational differences may not always be the core issue. 'The more I've seen and learned about our respective generations,' says Chip Conley, 'I realize that we often don't trust each other enough to actually share our respective wisdom.'

And this is because no matter which generation we are born into, we share the basic human need to be heard, trusted, respected, and appreciated. A Millennial with new ideas and enthusiasm wants to be heard and to get the validation that they are a valuable member of the team. Similarly, an older person wants their deep experience, accumulated wisdom, and organizational or political savvy to be recognized, utilized, and respected.

As President and Chief Operating Officer of real-estate company Optima, Tara Hovey oversees the US company's growth across its whole spectrum of operations. She came to the business through her family – her parents were active in residential development before she was born, founding Optima in 1978. But nothing was simply handed to her – she was expected to prove herself. And she did – in a big way. After earning an MBA from the University of Pennsylvania's Wharton School in 2012, Hovey did a stint at commercial real estate services company Cushman & Wakefield, where she underwrote nearly $1bn in debt and equity transactions.

When she took up her role at Optima in 2014, she found its multi-generational nature challenging. 'I was 30 years old and leading a construction company – a really high-stress, high-risk business,' she says.

'And it is architecture – male dominated. Construction – male dominated. Real estate development – male dominated. And we were doing really large deals.' Since joining the company, she has led the capitalization and financing of over $1bn in real estate, including construction financing for new developments, recapitalizations, and building dispositions.

How did she pull off these deals successfully?

'I had to negotiate with investors who were all men in their 60s and had been in the business a really long time,' she says. 'And some were just very rough and didn't necessarily have my values. But I had inherited them – the relationships already existed when I took over the leadership of the company.'

Hovey had to work to earn their respect in the negotiations and that took time, and the investors had to learn that she was the decision-maker, that there was no one else.

'I had a lot experiences like, "Wow, I didn't realize people were going to be like that or do things like that". But I had to accept those people for who they were.'

One early strategy was to make use of other people's expertise within the company. 'I made sure to work closely with my attorney and triple-check everything,' she says. Not because she didn't trust people, but because she wanted to be doubly if not triply sure of the situation and her facts.

And she tried to understand other people's points of view – though when it mattered, she held her ground. 'If something was important to me, I didn't give in and I tried to understand why a particular point was so important to them.'

But when someone was completely out of line with her values, she was firm. 'I had to draw the line when things were unacceptable. There was this gentleman I was negotiating with and someone on his team was mistreating people on my team, just very disrespectful things. I said, he cannot participate in this deal. And he's not allowed to talk to any of my employees because he's mistreating them. And he had to take his employee off the deal team. So there were hard conversations and hard calls to make.'

So Hovey has had to work hard to overcome being a young woman and to gain respect in an industry dominated by older men. She was determined to succeed and had the wisdom to listen and understand the point of view of the older people she was working with. And what shines through is her concern and respect for her team. She's engineering change by being competent, professional, authentic and yes, assertive, but always with empathy with the people involved.

This is instructive because by and large new-generation leaders like Tara Hovey do not believe in large-scale change driven from the top. Instead they want to change the nature of leadership and the workplace. And this means adopting a new more collaborative, inclusive, and empathetic leadership style.

In fact, all of the 50 New Leaders of Change in my study reject the leadership style of previous generations who more often than not embody the more autocratic, top-down leadership styles. Instead, many of the leaders I spoke with say they aspire to be a leader who is transparent, authentic, honest, and collaborative.

What does that mean, though, in practice?

Well, they want to lead with purpose, inclusivity, self-awareness, and emotional intelligence, they say, and enhance their interpersonal skills even further so they can be empathetic and inspiring leaders.

The contrast with the culture that exists at most traditional companies is stark, says Christy Lake, Chief People Officer at Twilio, a US cloud communications platform.

'I went from a large traditional company to a start-up with a culture of high empathy, high vulnerability. And shedding the professional persona and bringing your whole person to work was really new to me.'

This didn't exist at the traditional company she came from. 'There, everybody was buttoned up and it was a cover-your-ass mentality. You had friendships and relationships that were real, but when you walked into a meeting, you suited up.'

How different was it in her first start-up?

'Moving into start-up land, I learned vulnerability and being your authentic self,' she says. 'As leader, the more vulnerable you are, the more real you are, the more people want to work with you. And the more people trust you and the deeper the relationships you can have.'

She doesn't think her values have changed over the years, but her leadership style certainly has. 'As I reflect back to my first managerial experience, I had similar values, even though I didn't really know it was my natural approach. But as I got promoted to more senior levels, there was this implicit expectation that you need to have this professional executive presence, which means you are very buttoned up and you know your stuff.'

Now her executive presence really has changed. 'I can no longer not be my whole self, I can't have these discrete and different personas. I can't be protesting for Black Lives Matter in the weekend and then come in Monday morning meeting and say, "Hi gang, did you have a good weekend?" and not talk about what really matters to me.'

REFLECT ON WHO YOU NEED TO BE AT WORK

'I need to be in an environment where I feel like I can talk about the things that I'm passionate about or the things that I'm struggling with. And the more I can be vulnerable and let people know, the more people can support me and can help bolster me in different areas and can understand where I am.'

There are many other executives who share the same passion on this.

'I believe in transparency,' says Adnan Raza, CFO of PDF Solutions, a technology start-up. His leadership style reflects the priorities of his generation – transparency, being authentic, and solving leadership challenges collaboratively by engaging his team.

'On a scale of one to 10,' he says, 'I consider myself being 10 for openness, honesty, and transparency. Because you know what usually happens? When I am transparent on a particular problem I am having, like not being able to get funding or convincing investors, my team usually will sleep on it, and come back with creative solutions I may not have thought about.'

What does that look like?

'They will say, "I was thinking about our funding problem you mentioned – what if you pitch the data in a different way to investors?" Then I usually say, "Great, put it on a page."'

This style of leadership also works for Adrian Locher, the serial entrepreneur who has built several start-ups in the Artificial Intelligence space, including Merantix. 'Transparency and honesty always works,' he says.

'Honesty and authenticity always work for me because it boils down to trust. If you have very smart people, they deserve the truth. So if things are not going well, there's no reason to protect someone from reality.'

Really? No reason ever?

'I learned that I will not yield any good results from being protective. If you are trying to protect your kids from the bad out in the world by just keeping them home for the first 20 years, you're not going to bring up great citizens. For me, I view trust as the fundamental currency, not only in a personal and private relationship, but also in a working relationship.'

It's one thing to say that values such as transparency and humility matter to you, but it's another to practice them in a comprehensive way as a leader. But that's what Katie Koch of Goldman Sachs Asset Management has done.

'Last week I did some personal reflection and decided to role-model transparency and humility,' she says. It was a conscious and intentional exercise. 'I sent an email to all of our senior leaders in the business. I said, here are three things I did right, here are the three biggest mistakes I made over the last six months, and this is what I learned from them. I just sent it to everybody.'

What happened?

'And then people wrote back with their own mistakes and learnings.'

This was Koch's way of modeling humility. Helping the firm highlight what works, so they can share it, and what went wrong, so they can learn, propose new solutions, reiterate, and innovate.

HOW DO YOU MODEL HUMILITY?

At Goldman Sachs Asset Management, Koch says, 'you have to have the humility to know what you got wrong and that you're not perfect. And then have the growth mindset to address this.'[23]

This connection between humility and a growth mindset, or learning, is one of the reasons why Koch has built an investment culture around a set of shared values. 'We've chosen to organize ourselves around humility, transparency, collaboration, and diversity of thought.' She sees a clear connection between these values.

'Humility, for example, ultimately connects with having a growth mindset. Even the best investors can get stuff wrong. What is important is that we recognize and learn from these mistakes. Humility is the starting point of acknowledging that we don't know everything, and we can't do everything right.

'For example, we believe we are experts in identifying businesses to invest in for the long term. We have come to realize, however, that we are not good at timing markets or taking top-down macroeconomic views. As we reflected on this, we recognized the need to further develop our risk management tools to allow our portfolio managers to proactively control against such unintended biases and ensure stock selection, where we believe we have an edge, drives our risk and success at all times.'

I wonder aloud if living your values in this way is something only a few people will tackle. But Koch is adamant.

'Every company should have the humility to know what's not core to what you're trying to do every day and then really to own whatever it is that you have an edge in.'

Taking the issue of values a step further is Nikita Nosov, Global Operations Director at Flexport, the international freight forwarding company. He has been emotionally affected and inspired by events such as the global pandemic and the Black Lives Matter protests, and understands that these big social and emotional issues need to be discussed and processed in a safe community environment. He convened such a community and set up weekly meetings.

The purpose of such meetings? To enable authentic dialog, to build insights, and to process difficult emotional reactions.

'Since the start of the pandemic, we've established weekly meetings – there are five or six of us there,' he says. 'We spend a couple of hours having mindful conversations around these subjects. And I think that being able to have those sorts of dialog flourishes us.' Discussions and ideas flow in many different directions.

This evolution of conversation works in other areas, too, he says. 'I feel the same way about networking,' he says. 'When you meet people who share a genuine interest, the conversation can go in so many different directions you have no idea what the possibilities are, but they do exist.'

This is what happens when people show up in communities, teams, and organizations with authenticity and transparency, willing to share their emotions, fears, hopes, experiences, and ideas.

'When I meet with my community and we discuss these profound, deep, and complicated subjects that don't have a clear-cut solution, at least you're starting to put the pieces together,' Nosov says. 'Then you have these insights and you realize, "Oh, I should be thinking about it this way." Or "What is it I'm missing?" Or "What can I do to provide for that?" It helps you understand how to best spend your time and energy. I think that's the biggest thing.'

A belief in the power of community suffuses everything Nosov does, as with many next generation leaders. He first realized its power when he was a Peace Corps volunteer.

'I think this concept of community has been never more important in my life than today,' he says. 'But it wasn't clear to me until I lived in the Dominican Republic as part of my Peace Corps experience. It was like, "Wow, this is the power of community." And the power of these communal bonds is actually what makes the difference, what fulfills us.' He shakes his head at the enormity of it. 'Human connection is so key. So key.'

Nosov now lives in Seattle, Washington, where the first confirmed cases of Covid-19 in the US were reported in January 2020. For the following few months, Washington had the highest number of confirmed cases of any state in the country. And in May that year racial unrest erupted throughout the USA after the murder of George Floyd at the hands of the police. Such events, says Nosov, have reinforced the importance of community for him.

'I have actually been quite impacted by the unrest that's happened in recent years, the social unrest,' he says. 'I think a lot of people, like myself, are focusing on their community. For me, that means maintaining contact with that community and establishing some routine and to create stimulating, profound discussion around these important topics.' This is what he tries to focus on.

'That's what definitely stimulates me and it develops me as a leader in some ways. As someone who wants to grow these sorts of human bonds, create those spaces with my circle and other individuals where we can have deeper conversations on the important issues impacting us, our communities, our world, and our environment.'

In my experience, there are various competencies around communication, listening, understanding, and empathy that are key in forming meaningful relationships. Lindsey Crawford, Brand Strategy and Creative Consultant for Thermos, the consumer goods company puts it well.

'I believe if we come from a listening place and not feeling like we have all the answers, we can be open to learning,' she says.

'That doesn't mean we are soft, or we don't have an opinion. It is just that instead of approaching the challenge as a bulldog and breaking all the dishes around us, we can approach it like a fox. When a fox comes into an environment, they are listening, they are watching. They know what is around them.'

In a former role, Crawford's CEO acted as her mentor. 'I was willing to just observe and listen and watch, I learned so much so quickly,' she says. 'I would be in pitches with her and kind of study how she would organize her thoughts in a presentation format.'

THE IMPORTANCE OF RESILIENCE

A related facet that seems key here to the New Leaders of Change is resilience, the ability to bounce back after stressful situations. This is strengthened when you give and receive support – and listening plays a key role in this. So building positive relationships with people can make a difference in how resilient you are. You should try to connect with people who have a positive outlook and can make you laugh and help you. The more positive your relationships are, the better you will be able to face life's challenges.

We are profoundly social creatures – more than we know.[24]

Felicia Würtenberger, from Flooz, is another good example of a leader who is not afraid to invite employees to share and bring their whole selves to work as she facilitates personal, intimate dialogs between start-up leaders and their teams.

'Organizations are made up of human beings and, to lead people, you need to have good emotional intelligence and not be afraid to have hard conversations,' she says.

'For example, we have an engineer from Egypt, he has a wife and a new baby. They don't have a social network, don't speak German, and they have a lot of issues with their papers. Recently, the performance of this developer, of course, goes down. The tech lead was not happy at all and he was thinking this is not okay.'

Würtenberger realizes that forcing the engineer to focus on work won't make things better for him or for the tech lead.

'What I did was bring those two people in the room with me and then show this developer that the most important thing is that he is okay, that this whole situation at home is okay, because then he can focus again on work.'

It's a tricky challenge – some older managers think you need to leave your personal life at home.

'It is very sensitive when you are inquiring into people's personal lives and it requires a degree of psychological safety.[25] But I think to lead effectively, leaders need to have strong empathy. Some people feel like if they show empathy, they are seen as a weak leader, but that is the old model.'

Nico Arcino, Head of Strategic Partnerships at Kaiser Permanente, the US healthcare provider, says his view of empathy in leadership has been influenced by working in the healthcare sector. 'We spend an enormous amount of time and resources to carefully map our patient experiences in minute detail. We need a similar approach for personalizing employee experience.'

MANAGING CHANGE CHANGES YOU

Managing change within the company has transformed his leadership style. 'I really have seen a change in myself as leader as a result of managing multiple transformations,' he says. 'I'm a far more empathetic leader now.'

What does that mean in practical, day-to-day terms?

'I really spend a lot more time advising, enabling and mentoring than traditional blocking and tackling as a leader. I think more about how to motivate people and support them to get to where they want to be individually.'

How did this change in his style come about?

'I learned that team members are all complex individuals and we need to support, motivate, and coach at the individual level. So how do you do that? What are the tools to really identify what the individual needs are? It is like the personalization of the employee experience.'

As the new generation of leaders continue to take on more management and leadership roles, we can anticipate even greater visibility and permeation of their values. So expect to see more empathy in the workplace. It's been a long time coming.

It's clear talking to people like Würtenberger, Nosov, and Arcino that there's a new, yet ancient, vocabulary bubbling up when new-generation leaders talk about their leadership style, purpose, and values. This vocabulary invokes humanistic values, emotional awareness or empathy, humility, vulnerability, transparency, and the desire for deep connection in their personal and professional lives.

And this language is profoundly different from that used by older generations (see Table 4).

To some people it's a surprise that the very language we use can create misunderstandings between generations in the spotlight, highlighting the generation gap. When Würtenberger found herself working with an older leader at one point, she describes her experience as 'culture shock'. She was 'very surprised at the lack of empathy and curiosity the new leader exhibited toward the employees of the start-up'.

The CEO, aged 55, was very traditional in her outlook, she says. 'When I recommend things, she looks at me with a question mark in her eyes,' she says.

When Würtenberger suggested creating a vision, purpose, and set of values, the CEO simply said, 'We already have them.'

'I tried to explain to her what I meant and it was frustrating, I just couldn't describe it in a way she could understand. I felt like there is a language barrier, even though we speak the same language.'

Can she explain a bit more about that?

'It's just not about writing down a vision and set of values, you need to make connections with people at the human level.' In other words, it's about how you put those values into practice.

Würtenberger feels that sometimes she has to bridge the divide between the older-style CEO and the newer-style start-up team.

'As the HR leader, I have become the bridge between the CEO and the rest of the organization because people feel more comfortable talking to me rather than the CEO, even though we are a small start-up organization.'

How does the team feel?

Table 4: The new language of leadership

Leadership terms from the 20th Century	**Leadership terms for the mid 21st Century**
Lead, manage, direct, order, instruct	Inspire, motivate, empower, coach
Control-based, top-down, hierarchical leadership	Trust-based, bottom-up, horizontal, lateral, distributed, collective, co-leadership, servant leadership
Results, action, numbers oriented, analytical	Innovation, new ideas, iteration, creativity, analytical
Efficiency, effectiveness, it's not okay to fail	Innovation, reinvention, fail fast, learn fast
Only shares information if needed; 'knowledge is power'	Collaborate, co-create, 'We'. Radical transparency; 'none of us is as smart as all of us'
Staff, subordinate, resource	Colleagues, whole human beings, team members
Values experience, track-record, qualifications, achievements, specific expertise	Values attitude, creativity, self-awareness, ability/desire to learn, curious, adaptable, collaboration, culture-fit, potential
IQ is sole measure of intelligence	IQ and EQ are equally important
IQ: logical, analytical, rational, factual, technical know-how, critical thinker, independent thinker	EQ: empathy, compassion, vulnerability, humility, self/emotional awareness, awareness of others' emotions, relational
Uses cognitive data as information	Uses expressed emotions as information
Decisive, no need for consultation, discussion or consensus	Solicits input, feedback, and invites different perspectives to the discussion
Power kept to self	Shares power, empowers people
Leverage technology to make things 'better, faster, cheaper'	Leverage technology for innovating new streams of business, innovation, disruption, transformation

'The team feels lost,' she says. 'There are a lot of decisions being made, but we don't know what is going on and there is no transparency. I tried to bring the issues up to the CEO and recommend some actions – the only thing she said was, "It's not always democracy."'

As a result of her experiences, Würtenberger feels the need for a new definition of leadership.

'Sometimes I feel these leaders have an old definition of leadership in their minds and they think they have to lead this way; but that's not compatible with being human, being vulnerable, and making human connections.'

Andrea Ruotolo, working in the heavily technical utilities field, found that her way of building a community of creative people within her company soon created its own momentum. 'My current role is about starting a new unit in the company from grass-roots level,' she explains. 'I am an intrapreneur where I am developing a community of innovators and disruptors that will create the future of the company.'

Then a pause.

'I think I was preparing for this role for all my 36 years.'

Clearly she loves her job, but it hasn't been easy. 'It has been a journey. I started as an influencer without any direct reports and very quickly I started to create a momentum inside the company. As we exchanged ideas, people wanted to join the team and things started happening suddenly.'

Interest grew within the company and the community soon reached 60 people. 'Our mission is to accelerate the transformation away from the central systems we have today,' she says. 'We need more local energy systems to ensure local people have their power on. I come from Argentina – I have experienced first-hand what it is to have power outages every week. So now we have 60 people committed to this mission.'

Along the way they also have the challenge of building more resilient energy systems in the face of new climate conditions and cyber-attacks.

It's been hard for a new generation leader within a large organization to change the way things are done without backing. Luckily Ruotolo had support.

'I had very supportive leaders,' she says, 'who were hands-off and they let me experiment and go through the discovery process. They know I had the passion and I didn't need much guidance… all I needed was freedom to make it happen.'

And creating communities was the key. 'I was able to tap into the collective intelligence of the company and develop this community with a passionate mission... we were able to hit some magic.'

After a year, they brought in another manager with a more structured approach. Ruotolo thinks this was the right person at the right time. 'This is exactly what we need at this stage,' she says. 'We were given more funding. Also, we expanded the scope of the group and added networks in addition to Distributed Energy.' It was an acknowledged success for the group.

'The company has never done anything like this before. I started a movement and now the company is putting a lot of support, funding, and faith in what we are doing. So it is a big responsibility for me, for the team, and for the company, in terms of shareholders and so on.'

Following the success in her own division, Ruotolo is reaching out to other areas of the company. 'We are also engaging other groups across the company. We had a meeting with 25 business development leaders and discussed how they connect clients with what we are doing, how can we engage clients.'

In the same way she is reaching out to others in the company, people are also reaching out to her – including many from the newest generation in the business, Generation Z.

'The new generation of Gen Zs are constantly reaching out to me and they want to transform their careers and be part of this movement,' she says.

'I am starting to take on more of a mentoring role and I really like that. This whole experience has helped me discover that there's a calling for me, part of that calling is also about helping people grow, develop, and reach higher levels in the organization. So it is all coming together.'

So change is happening fast, but not as part of some overall top-down plan. Change is emerging, rapidly, built by the communities of people passionate to see things happen.

I recall Ruotolo describing herself as an intrapreneur – an entrepreneur working inside a company to transform it, helping it to become more entrepreneurial. And as a representative of this new generation of intrapreneurs, she's stepping up, speaking out, and making a difference.

But in fact all the people I've interviewed have shared these characteristics – together with many others. They demonstrate confidence, commitment, and courage in the face of adversity. They are open, transparent, and demonstrating what it takes to be purpose-driven. They are showing us what is possible when it comes to leading change.

Venetia Bell of GIB Asset Management is another good example of the New Leaders of Change. She certainly doesn't think the way to manage change is to take a template or a checklist and try to implement it.

'I don't have a single approach to leading change and transformation,' she says. 'It is quite eclectic depending on the nature of the challenges.'

What's interesting to me as an outsider is that Bell isn't simply disregarding the valuable knowledge contained within the various models of change management.

'I have worked with all the dominant methods like stakeholder alignment, political influence, developing change agents, role models, and so on,' she says. 'But it's a bit boring and it doesn't grab people too much.'

She believes inspiration and motivation are more important than following a prescribed change program. 'Lately, I have been taking a more external and partnership approach to changing the perceptions and educating people about the kind of transformation journey we are embarking on. I am having external speakers to come in, talk about their transformation journey, and inspire the team.'

If people can see what they are trying to do, she says, they will understand and engage more with the process.

'As I am trying to align the bank around the principles of responsible investing, I am partnering with external organizations. We are doing really interesting partnerships with the World Economic Forum, International Committee of the Red Cross, World Bank, and a few others. It is a great example where you can use the power of external voices to push the organization internally.'

She smiles, remembering some of the successes.

'When you are partnering with great names and amazing people, others want to get involved and want to get behind the change initiatives.'

Now Bell finds her team is being recognized by the partner organizations for the work they are doing in responsible investing. 'The team can see that external recognition and validation we are getting for the work we are doing.' That's a big bonus, she says.

What we're seeing today across the world, in companies of every size, is that the communities driven by Millennial-style leadership are far different from the regimented environments that have long defined workplaces. In the past employees had little to no flexibility, had to do what they were told, and had to divide themselves into a professional and a personal self.

In the very near future we will see more people lead with emotional intelligence and empathy, more people lead with purpose, and more people seeing their employees as whole people rather than resources. The New Leaders of Change are here. ■

“Once I realized that this was an almost impossible mission that a lot of smart people had been trying to do for a long time, I was interested and I said yes.

Donna See
CEO
Xora Innovation

Chapter 5

A CALL TO ADVENTURE

Having the courage to leap and take action

It's early Monday morning and Trevor Campbell is sitting in a commuter private jet on his way to Santa Barbara, California, from San Francisco. He is stressed.

'My first day in my new role as the leader of a 15-person team. I am already stressed out. All I could think of was to call my mentor, who is not part of the company I worked for. And it's Monday morning, I haven't even walked into the office yet.'

Campbell's boss had made a surprise trip to the San Francisco office a few days before and told him that his manager had been removed with immediate effect. Campbell would have to replace her and show up at the Santa Barbara office the following Monday morning.

'She really blindsided me,' he says, 'and said I want you to be the head of West Coast sales. This was really a difficult stage for me, because at the time I had five people in San Francisco, but in Santa Barbara there were 15 sellers doing $12m a quarter.'

He didn't have time for any proper preparation. 'I really didn't have anybody who briefed me or told me how to face 15 people as their leader. Some of them were older than me. One of them was 45 years old and here I am, 27 years old, and I'm going to be his boss.'

For the next two years, Campbell, now VP of Sales, Asia Pacific, for Tapjoy, the mobile advertising company, commuted to Santa Barbara. 'I would go down there 60 times in one year. It was nerve wracking for sure to be thrown into such a big role suddenly. I wish I could tell you I had a plan, but I really didn't honestly.'

As Campbell discovered, leadership takes courage. The leadership journey requires the courage to take the leap into new, uncertain, and challenging situations.

For the new leaders of the 21st century, the call to adventure is irresistible. They are courageous, optimistic, flexible, and quick to take decisions. They are stepping up to the challenge, personally and professionally. As they accept the call to adventure, they are embarking on a transformational journey, coming to an understanding of themselves as leaders, as well as of the world around them. Transformation of the self and of the world naturally occur when we have the courage to go beyond our current understanding and awareness of ourselves, of our role as leaders.

The leaders in this book also understand the fact that you cannot think your way through this change. You have to learn to lean into it and experience it for yourself.

Johnny Luk, who was born in Hong Kong and lived in the Netherlands and Germany before moving to the UK at 10 years old, received his first leadership lesson in his teens. Now a Senior Associate at Global Counsel, the advisory firm, a columnist for *Al Jazeera*, and the former CEO of the National Association of College and University Entrepreneurs, a non-profit company, he traces his leadership success back to his teens.

'I was one of the very few Chinese people in my high school and I found myself really struggling with my identity as a British-Chinese,' he says. 'I found the best way to escape my dilemma was to throw myself into sport and joined the rowing club, which didn't distinguish success through appearances or background. I trained hard for a singular goal and hoped by the end I could prove to myself I was a "somebody".'

So when there was an opportunity to step into being the captain of the rowing club, Luk jumped at it.

'It was an incredible opportunity. This particular rowing club had really deteriorated over a period of time. The director of coaching had left. Because of that I had space and opportunity to try things slightly out of the box.

'I created a public engagement campaign to get more funding and better conditions for rowers.' Soon they attracted more students to join the club.

'What then happened was we competed in the British championships in 2008 and we hit a big wave and we sank. We lost a boat worth £36,000 ($50,000). It's on YouTube, it's gone viral. I was a laughing stock.'

He shudders at the memory and what it meant to him.

'I was the Chinese guy that sank the boat, partly because I removed some of the inside parts of the boat to make it lighter but they were actually quite important for keeping the boat afloat.'

In spite of this setback, Luk carried on rowing. 'We trained really hard and in 2009 we actually won the British title and that meant so much to me. And then in 2016, they named the boat after me.'

LEARNING BY DOING

He says he learned about leadership by actually doing it. 'My style of leadership since then has always been very collegiate. I don't subscribe to the command and control way. I think it's all about empowerment.'

So the new generation of leaders we're talking about here, the New Leaders of Change, are purposeful, optimistic, and possess what Professor Carol Dweck calls a growth mindset (Dweck, 2006). They are constant learners and see every challenge as an opportunity to grow.

The New Leaders of Change are also revolutionary, in a very personal way. Like Trevor Campbell, they are called to action and they take the leap into the unfamiliar with courage. Yes, there is some fear, but more often than not it's their curiosity and openness to adventure that prevails.

'I was never the person to say no to a new adventure, or experience,' says Nirupa Chander, Country Managing Director, Singapore, for Hitachi ABB Power Grids. 'There's nothing really to lose. You just have to say "yes", even when you're a little bit doubtful about whether you will succeed or not.'

She recalls the moment she overcame her fears and just said 'yes'.

'I had just moved to Australia from India to secure a sizable contract for my company with a value of $15m. After the deal was closed, I was asked to lead the delivery of the project.'

It was a complex, large-scale project, working with a cross-functional team and involved managing factories in different parts of the country.

'I was terrified, but I said yes,' she says.

'Here I was, this 20-something young woman who recently migrated from India, storming through the factories and telling everyone what they needed do and how they were going to work with the client.' She shakes her head in amazement.

Courage to embrace the personal challenge of leadership, like that shown by Trevor Campbell, Johnny Luk, and Nirupa Chander, is a prerequisite for great leadership in the face of volatility, uncertainty, complexity, and ambiguity. While courage may have many facets, at the heart of courageous leadership is the willingness to take decisive action, take risks, and step up to the challenge amid uncertainty – to tear down the walls of your comfort zone and, almost, to sideline your personal psychological safety.

This is not an easy task. If it were easy to embrace personal and professional change in the face of uncertainty, more people would. But our brains are wired to avoid danger and seek safety and security.

This doesn't seem to be the case with Donna See, CEO at Xora Innovation in Singapore. 'After seven years, I was feeling finally settled down in Manhattan, New York, and had developed a huge network both professionally and personally,' she says. 'I ended up loving everything and thought I would never leave.'

Then she got a call from a headhunter. 'It was more like a mystery call because they would not tell me who they were representing.'

She told the headhunter, 'Well, if you can't tell me who your client is, I am not interested.'

They finally told her who was recruiting and for what job. She really didn't think it was something she wanted to leave New York for. But she kept thinking.

'At some point I realized this was an impossible job in an impossible country. They had been trying to do early-stage science investing and commercialization since 2007, for 13 years, and they had thrown a lot of money at it. And it was based in Singapore.'

Then something strange clicked. 'Once I realized that this was an almost impossible mission that a lot of smart people had been trying to do for a long time, I was interested and I said yes.'

The new generation of leaders exhibits a bias for action in the face of challenging situations, or as Donna See calls it, 'impossible missions'.

They're willing to put themselves out there, overcome their fear of the unknown and of failure, and to take risks. They have the courage and resilience to navigate their organization through the unprecedented challenges of the 21st century.

PURPOSE AND PROFIT: CREATING SHARED VALUE

But a sense of adventure and an appetite for challenge are not the only factors driving the new generation of leaders. Over the past few years, there has been much discussion on the purpose-driven approach to business and leadership. The momentum behind this is the preference of younger leaders to work for purpose-driven companies and for finding a greater sense of meaning in their work and life.

According to American Express research *Redefining the C-Suite: Business the Millennial Way* (and there's a raft of similar research all over the web), Millennials are ambitious and motivated, while also seeking work with a purpose beyond simply earning money.[26] Here are just a couple of numbers that struck me from this research:

- 62 per cent of Millennials want to be known for making a positive difference in the world, compared with 52 per cent of Generation X;

- 55 per cent care about what family and friends think of their career, against 43 per cent of Generation X.

So they aspire to build organizations that succeed in the marketplace by earning the respect, trust, and commitment of their people, customers, communities, and investors. Don't worry, though, this isn't an abdication of their fiduciary duty to the firm and to shareholders. The new generation of leaders focus on building businesses for purpose and profit to serve a diverse set of stakeholders and society more broadly.

When Tara Hovey and her brother took over the leadership of Optima, their family's real-estate business, the first thing they did was define the purpose and a set of core values for the company, engaging all employees in the process.

'Take away all the accomplishments on my bio and ask what are the leadership experiences that I am really emotionally attached to,' she tells me. I can't guess. 'Going through the process of developing a purpose statement and set of core values for the company,' she says. 'Asking the question, what do we want to be?'

Her words trip over themselves as she recalls the process. 'It was like peeling back the onion and uncovering what we are and what is really there at the core of the company. It was very inspirational. We had everybody provide input and have that clarity. It was a way of empowering people and giving them voice.'

The activity represented a complete change of leadership style for the company. 'When the business started, all the decisions would go to my father,' she says. 'Then there were veterans who have been there for 30 years.' They certainly knew the purpose and core values implicitly, but it was never clearly articulated.

'When my brother and I took over the company, we were hiring a lot of new people. We didn't want to be a bottleneck for decisions. We wanted to empower everyone at every level of the organization to be making all the day-to-day decisions in alignment with our purpose and core values.'

She was really clear why they were doing this. 'So every architect, designer, construction superintendent, and every person in company could clearly articulate the purpose and core values.'

LIFE IN A PURPOSE-DRIVEN ORGANIZATION

In a purpose-driven organization, leaders and employees have a shared view of their mission. They feel connected to each other and there is a strong sense of belonging. Grounded in this purpose, teams collaborate to weather multiple storms while setting their organizations up for continued success.

'We found a very high level of consensus among executives that purpose matters, and a widespread belief that it has positive effects on key performance drivers,' says Valerie Keller, Global Lead of EY Beacon Institute in the report *The Business Case for Purpose*.[27] She adds that companies who clearly articulate their purpose enjoy higher growth rates and higher levels of success in transformation and innovation initiatives.

At Google, Banks Baker, Head of Global Partnerships, works with Millennials and Gen Z leaders from all over the world. And he has a phrase for what Google is trying to do: North Star. 'Google works very hard to sustain a North Star on how it sees its purpose, its mission, how it sees itself bringing value to customers, how it sees itself bringing value to society,' he says.

'I think those are the things that help organizations weather any crisis. Focusing on your core purpose can help you weather economic cyclical trends, unexpected social or political crises (like Covid-19), and any other disruptions. Your core purpose creates a glue at the base of the business and binds everybody together.'

Before joining Google, Baker worked for a start-up. 'It started as a very successful business. However, it didn't have a core purpose, a reason for being,' he says. 'The founder made that business, the founder walked away with several hundred million dollars. The next person in line probably walked away with a few million dollars. It was all about making a founder as much money as possible.'

Then the problems started. 'As the business got larger and larger, and we got up from eight people to 450 people, the wheels just started coming off. There was no real way to make effective decisions. There was no clear star on where we were going.'

Having a clearly defined purpose, then, can help people overcome most challenges. Katie Koch, Co-head of Fundamental Equity at Goldman Sachs Asset Management, says purpose-driven leadership has helped her in many difficult turnaround situations.

'I think you have to set the right tone, a shared purpose, the right set of shared values,' she says. 'You have to keep coming back to that.'

Why?

'The markets will go up, the markets will go down. The environment will be good or bad. You're hired by people, you will get fired by people. You'll get some stuff right and get some stuff wrong. But you have to have some set of shared purpose and values to keep coming back to.'

HR professional Felicia Würtenberger, who constantly takes the pulse of new generations of leaders, agrees that a sense of purpose is crucial.

'The young generation of people, Millennials, Gen Z, we all pretty much agree that companies we work for, start-up or traditional companies, need to be a good place to work. We all need to understand the purpose – why we are doing the things we do every day.'

Again I ask why?

'I think this is missing in lots of companies, including in the start-up I am working in which was acquired by two traditional companies as a joint venture. We have a vision somewhere written, but it's not transported into the organization.'

Würtenberger says one way leaders can help people understand what they're doing is through creating a narrative or story around the company. 'I think leaders can do a lot with creating a connection between company vision, purpose, values, and employees by using stories, pictures, videos, and emotions. Stories about people told by people, whether it's customers, partners, employees, and bring people back into the center.'

So the next generation of leaders is not only willing to answer the call to adventure, but they demand a sense of purpose.

Someone who illustrates this combination of drives is Linda Dörig. When her call to adventure came, she was stationed in Burkina Faso in West Africa, working for Gebana, the international fair and sustainable trade company.

The company collaborates with thousands of local farmers and customers across the world to sell products directly via their online shop. 'Burkina Faso is the biggest company that Gebana has,' she says. 'We have a factory where we process cashew nuts and dried mangos. And so we have over 600 people working in the factory.'

At the time, the CEO in Burkina Faso was the sole senior manager and had been there for 15 years. All the suppliers were linked to him, but there was a problem.

'The company was not doing very well,' says Dörig. And it was a problem that everyone could see. 'I was not at all involved in the operations of the factory, but was aware of the issues like everyone else.'

The corporate office decided to replace the CEO and called Dörig. They said, 'You are already on site and maybe you can do it as an interim until we recruit someone.'

She couldn't believe what she was hearing. 'I thought, these guys are crazy. They have no clue what was going on down here. They just know the peak of the iceberg, they didn't know what was going on below that.'

But head office persisted, asking, 'Could you do it for a while?'

'I thought this is completely crazy,' she says, 'because it is a big company and there are many people and they are all linked to the current CEO. You take the CEO out, you don't know what will happen. Financially the company was in a bad situation and everything was really difficult.'

Nevertheless, she considered the offer carefully. 'I thought about the people who worked there, mostly ladies,' she says. 'These ladies do not have other opportunities or chances, they can't read or write. I always made a point of mingling with them, I ate lunch with them and the farmers.'

And she stopped fighting for a moment. 'I thought, what will happen to them if I don't take this position? They probably will not find someone else immediately. So I thought, someone has to step in and fix the current issues – otherwise, the company will go under.'

'I HAVE TO DO IT'

No one was sure if the factory might have to close, especially in the face of various legal actions that emerged. 'Everything was insecure. I just thought, "I have to do it… I will do it."'

I asked her why?

'I decided, okay, I have to do it because these people have to be able to continue working. And I just thought, I have to take it over.'

A pause.

'I think this is when I felt this responsibility for people, when I took the lead.'

In this way, Linda Dörig simultaneously answered the call to adventure and found her purpose.

She's not the only one who works this way.

'I need to have a super-strong "why",' says Andrea Ruotolo. 'Something that is coming from my heart and my mind.'

Why does she put it like that?

'I discovered throughout my life that when I align my heart and my mind, I can bring my full, undivided energy to the work, and that's when I'm able to achieve the most. It's like what people call a "flow" state, when you're completely absorbed in what you're doing. Yeah, that connection with my heart, the sense of what matters and what is right, is very critical for me to be able to bring my full self to the project.'

And I thought about this: the root of the word 'courage' is 'cor', the Latin for heart. So the key to developing courage is to know what is in your heart. In other words, to be honest with yourself.

Throughout my interviews, I heard stories where leaders continually aligned their hearts and minds with their actions. They described their core values, such as being authentic with themselves and others; getting involved in a deep and personal way with their employees, partners, and customers; and being honest about their feelings and speaking up when something didn't feel right.

Maybe you're the same. When your purpose and values are clear, and you understand the meaning and significance of your work, you will have the words in your heart to be authentic, to be real, and to speak up. You will never have to wrestle with the question, 'What if ...?' Because you will know what is in your heart, and you will act on it.

You will be filled with courage.

Andrea Ruotolo describes getting in touch with her 'why' as a journey of discovery. 'Learning where and how I can make my greatest contribution has been a self-discovery process and it has taken me setting aside time for self-assessment and reflection.'

The journey began when Ruotolo, a Fulbright scholar with a PhD in energy and environmental policy, was a young leader working for New York State Smart Grid Consortium. There she found herself working in a group of some of the most important stakeholders in the US driving energy change, most of whom were senior to her.

'I was sitting in a meeting with over 70 stakeholders who were making decisions about how policy and regulations should be part of shaping the new energy future in New York State,' she says. There were CEOs of major corporations, utilities, stakeholder group representatives, subject matter experts, and public officials.

'As I listened to them, I started to see where gaps and problems they were identifying aligned with solutions I had been thinking about, and things I was passionate about doing.'

That alignment of thinking of practical solutions and feeling passionate about the potential to help others gave her a strong 'why', a connection of heart and mind, and she quickly went into action.

She and her husband, who also works in the energy industry, spent nights and weekends working out plans on a whiteboard they hung on the wall in their living room. They decided to start their own company to help address some of the gaps in the market that surfaced during her work in New York. 'I saw it as a great opportunity,' she says. They named their entrepreneurial project UpGrid, and began consulting to larger companies and utilities throughout the Americas, focusing on smart grid technologies and Distributed Energy Systems (DES), such as microgrids, distributed solar power, and battery energy storage systems.

The sense of purpose that drove Ruotolo to found her own company is essential to her. 'One of the things I've learned about myself is that when I really care about getting something done, I can be incredibly persistent, and overcome obstacles others might see as impossible. But to feel that level of commitment, it needs to be both practical and it needs to serve a larger purpose. I need to have a super-strong "why?" that is coming from my heart as well as my mind.'

This wasn't something she found out about herself early in her life, she says. 'It's been a journey of understanding myself and how best I can serve other people. Because I am always asking myself, "What is in my heart?" or "What is my mission?"'

She is also clear who she is doing this for. 'Shouldn't everything we do take very serious consideration for the wellness of the future generations? Shouldn't we do all we can to ensure they have a healthy and clean environment to thrive in, and safe, reliable infrastructure that will be sustainable for many more generations to come?'

Talking with Andrea Ruotolo, I am captivated by her positive energy, her passion, and her intellectual capacity. She's happy to share how getting clear on her vision, mission and 'why' is a key milestone for her. However, she's also aware that she needs to balance her own passion for her work with meeting people where they are, to enlist, motivate, and bring others along on the journey at their own pace.

'Once I was clear on my vision and mission, I became super-focused on making progress and driving things forward,' she says. 'I approached situations with a lot of energy, passion, and with a "let's make this happen" attitude. However, I discovered that my attitude of "we have to get this done no matter what" did not always resonate with everyone, and I gained a much better understanding of how important it is to respect the different perspectives we all have, of the right ways, and the right pace to bring about change.'

She's learned a lot in this regard, to make sure she connects with the many kinds of people who are involved in her projects and to make sure she doesn't leave people behind. 'I became much more aware of other people's motivations and needs and began asking myself: where is this person at right now with their personal and professional lives? What is their feeling toward change in their sector – positive, negative, neutral? What is motivating them?'

It was a struggle initially and a big lesson. 'I learned to be a balanced leader and started to observe, listen, and have much more empathy for my team members. I became much more aware and conscious about why a certain team member may be sad, anxious, or stressed. What are their thoughts and concerns? What is their "why", and how can we connect with that deeper source of motivation?'

The acceptance that different people are motivated by different things is something that comes with experience.

'To succeed in cultural or organizational transformation, having all the key people aligned is so critical, so critical,' says Ruotolo. 'And I think having that alignment starts first in the heart, and then in our mindsets, and both of those two need to connect. It's really critical. I think we need to take more time in understanding who is the other person behind the resumé, behind their achievements and that initial presence and presentation of themselves.'

So first and foremost, the new leaders of the 21st century are purpose-driven. They want to know why they're doing what they're doing. And discovering their 'why', at some point during their journey enables them to find the courage, motivation, and inspiration to take risks, overcome barriers, and march towards their North Star.

Stepping up to the challenge of leadership in this way, before you change your mind, requires courage and trust that you will be able to push through obstacles and create change for people, organizations, and yourself.

But ultimately, you will learn to lead on the job and build your 'character' through making mistakes, suffering setbacks, and also celebrating successes. This is the kind of experiential learning you can't get from an MBA or a degree.

So how can you as a new leader benefit from your peers' experience? I believe that as you listen to their stories, you will become more conscious of the process of leadership and the journey. As you come to understand the process, the character-building challenges, and the courage needed to take bold action, you can reflect on your own leadership journey, gain more confidence, and unlock the agency you need to go forward.

Where are you on your leadership journey? Taking the leap? Learning lessons on the journey? Or can you see the end of the road and are curious about what is next?

How does where you are on your journey influence the way you lead?

It starts when you look in the mirror. ■

The NEW LEADERS of CHANGE

PART III: CHANGE

THE HUMAN EXPERIENCE REVOLUTION

“I think sometimes I forgot about myself and would give 100 per cent to my people and give 100 per cent to the clients. At some point I kind of lost myself… I had to change myself and learn to bring more balance into my life.

Debbie O'Neill
VP Domestic Partnerships
Honey

Chapter 6

LEADERSHIP IS A JOURNEY NOT A DESTINATION

How the New Leaders of Change embark on the inner journey of self-growth

When Adrian Locher successfully sold the company he co-founded, he found himself with several options. He could continue with his entrepreneurship activities – start another company, invest in a joint venture, and quickly move into the next thing. Or he could do nothing and enjoy being financially secure at a young age and spend more time with his kids.

Locher decided to take a sabbatical and reflect on what he should do next to bring meaning and purpose into his life.

'I realized this is now a big milestone I have achieved,' he says. 'And I really want to spend some time thinking before I move on to the next thing, because I knew myself enough that I can fall in love with things quite quickly.' He laughs – he knows himself too well.

'My biggest concern was that I would actually just do the next and most probable thing and not the most important thing. Now I had the means to focus on the important thing.' But he needed to find out what that was.

'I was quite bored with the industry I was in and I really didn't see a purpose in what I was doing any longer. I had the strong need to find something that is more important, more purposeful to work on to spend my life. Perhaps it really was as simple as spending a lot more time with my kids.'

So he allowed himself time to work out his priorities.

'If I wanted to do a new project, I want to be sure that it's a worthy cause. I forced myself into a year of sabbatical. I did not allow myself to sign any contract to do any larger investment – I wanted to basically spend time studying.'

He went to Stanford University to study and lived in San Francisco for six months.

Over time, he developed a way of working out what he wanted to do. 'Eventually I developed a framework that helped me choose my next steps,' he says. 'I asked myself three questions to narrow down and filter the opportunities I was seeing.' And he shared them with me.

1. What is it that you really believe about the future? What will the world look like in 25-50 years? What will be the most important topics and issues?

2. What really fascinates and attracts you?

3. Where can you actually provide some added value with the background you have?

'I spent several months learning and reflecting on these questions, which ultimately led me to AI and my current portfolio of start-ups in the AI area.' Nowadays Locher is CEO of Merantix, the Artificial Intelligence venture studio he founded, and he's very happy helping other new leaders to learn how to navigate their leadership journey and self-growth.

The leader's journey is a deeply personal exploration of understanding who you are and how you need to evolve to be worthy of leading. Capable, fully competent leaders are always evolving. They are never fully satisfied and never feel that their curiosity is satiated.

Adrian Locher's courage and commitment to his leadership journey reveal the importance of critical self-reflection and continuous, deep learning. Self-reflection is the practice of thinking about and learning from one's experiences – successes, failures, disappointments, and regrets. It is also a process of examining our biases, assumptions, and the beliefs that influence how we make meaning out of those experiences.

Critical self-reflection takes time, it is not a process that can be done in the middle of your daily activities. Locher's decision to take a sabbatical versus diving into a new venture allowed him to reflect and learn.

His insights also reveal another channel for self-development: working with a sounding board. Not subscribing to the cliché that leadership is a lonely business, the leaders in this study have often turned to mentors, coaches, and allies to help them overcome obstacles. Although the idea of having a single mentor or a coach is becoming outdated, it seems, I have often been told of the importance of building a team around you.

This team is usually a constellation of strategic supporters – peers, mentors, sponsors, coaches, and allies, both internal and external to the company. And these trusted relationships can be formal or informal. They have the right credentials, know-how, and passion – to mentor, support, or advocate for you and your causes, even when you are not physically present.

Sometimes they can show up unexpectedly to guide us through adversity and assist us in becoming stronger and better, transformed by our leadership journey.

Think about it. What successful leader accomplished their status all by themselves?

'A one-mentor model can be self-limiting at times,' says Nirupa Chander, Managing Director, Singapore, for Hitachi ABB Power Grids. 'In my career, fortunately I have had the support of many well-wishers and guides. Sometimes these mentors were family and at other times my managers or other senior leaders in the organization.'

The key is to build a network – a wide one, she says. Don't limit yourself to just a few people. You should spread links, weak or strong, all around you as you actively build your own support team.

Internal mentors, sponsors, and allies with strong relationships across the business can be critical in making connections. They can recommend you, connect you with other leaders who are experts in the relevant subject area, or open doors to other opportunities.

Chander says this happened to her. 'One of the leaders on the project adopted me and watched me through the sidelines. He knew I was capable and he had the unique ability to get the best out of people.' Her mentor believes we can all do more than we think we can. Importantly, she says, he also believes we can do more than other people think we can.

'He recommended me for a very large-scale and complex leadership role and he fought for me with other managers to secure the role for me. He said, "She is new, she is green, but she is going to do a good job."' He was sure of it.

'When others pushed back because I was so young and inexperienced, he said, "Well, that's okay. Let her burn her fingers."'

What did she make of that?

'The way I interpreted this was, it is difficult, but it is okay to fail. And he was right, it was tough. But I thought, I am just going to give it my best shot.'

She knew she could also ask for help and guidance if she needed to. Because asking for help and guidance is not a sign of weakness, it's a sign of good leadership. Chander is convinced that you can't be expected to be proficient at every skill or know everything. Mentors can give you the confidence you need to overcome any fears you have or any false sense of being incompetent.

RELATIONSHIPS HELP IN SURPRISING WAYS

Trevor Campbell, now regional VP of Sales at Tapjoy, was daunted when he was first appointed as leader of a big team. He knew he was inexperienced in some areas. But the relationships he forged with more senior leaders helped him to perform.

'I know the subject matter really well,' he says. 'I can sell the product myself in my sleep and I did hire and manage a small group that I felt very good about. I had some confidence from that, but I didn't even know how to forecast revenue. My director, she did that usually… I would roll up my numbers to her.'

What happened?

'I called on one of the VPs I knew and asked, how do you forecast revenue? I've been lucky that I've always been really good at having relationships with senior people at the company, like real relationships. And I always called on them.'

The most accomplished leaders often surround themselves with amazing, inspiring, and strong people as allies and coaches, or mentors and supporters. Without them, their legacies may be very different.

Surrounding herself with mentors is exactly the strategy of Erika Velazquez, AVP Digital Ecosystem Manager of the Electrification Business at ABB in Switzerland.

'I always have two or three mentor relationships,' she says, 'because I seek out a mentor for a specific challenge I am working on. Once I identify the right person who can help me with a specific goal, then I reach out to them and begin the conversation.'

How does that outreach process work?

'It's a little bit like dating,' she says. 'Sometimes after one or two meetings, if I feel we don't really click and I am not able to connect, I realize this isn't really working. And in other cases, the relationship really takes off.'

Do you only have coaches for immediate problems?

'I also have long-term role models whom I have known over 10 years and they have really helped me grow professionally and personally.'

Sometimes coaches also emerge in your team, if you slow down and listen – they have deep functional and technical expertise you may not possess as the leader. They can help you gain valuable insights into how they do their jobs, tackle challenges, and find innovative solutions. This requires leaders to be open to learning, having the ability for deep listening and empathy, and to create an environment of respect. This seems to come naturally to the new generation of leaders.

Linda Dörig, whose leadership journey began in West Africa where – as a young, white woman from Switzerland – she turned around a complicated and difficult company, puts it much the same way. 'I'm very focused on people. I communicate with people and I listen to the people and I try to motivate and enable the people. I don't do that as a strategy or plan. For me it was a very natural process, to focus on the people.'

So if you can listen to your team, knowing the functional or technical aspects of your business becomes less critical. 'I don't know how to best crack cashew nuts,' she says, 'but these people have been doing it for so many years. They know much better than I do. So I have to ask them, listen to them. They will have plenty ideas if I let them communicate ideas on how to make things better.'

The knowledge transfer process, however, is two-way, she says.

'I also know some things about optimizing processes and things like that, so putting my know-how and their ideas together with them was how I approached the challenges of Burkina Faso.'

She believes it's important to trust the members of your team – though this can be tough in a time of business change, uncertainty, and leadership transition. 'Of course, it was helpful that I was already there for two years and I knew the people,' she says. 'I had a good feeling about who to trust. But it was a very divisive time, because people were teaming up with the former CEO and there were difficulties with trust.'

How did that situation work out?

'There was one French employee, he was also sent from the Swiss headquarters a few months before. He is a finance specialist for 25 years and he had been in West Africa for 35 years. I told headquarters, I need one person to trust and I trust this colleague. So he became my finance director. From there, we had to recruit the right people and let go of the wrong people.'

What happened next?

'This was basically the start. Engaging people, getting their ideas to fix the problems and motivating the people to continue to work for us.'

She thinks you shouldn't try to hide anything from the stakeholders. 'The suppliers, I had to ensure they continued their partnership with us. I did that through very open and transparent communications.'

What do you say to someone, in practical terms, in a situation like that?

'I said, "Look, you all know the problems. We have to fix the problems. It is easier if you help me. And those of you who continue to do the wrong things, I will not hesitate to take the right action. I will try to make it better for all of you, but I cannot fix all the problems alone."'

She found that people responded well. They stepped up and actually wanted to contribute to the survival of the business. It was in everyone's interests.

'It was really helpful that I lived in the town with the people and established a relationship with the workers, farmers, and suppliers. When I travel to a different country or culture, I don't stay within an expert community. I lived locally, I was very used to being in their homes or in their families.'

In this way Dörig rebuilt a successful team in difficult circumstances.

'All the people who ended up staying with Burkina Faso became my allies and supporters,' she says. 'Together we were able to accomplish a lot and turn the company around.'

Her intentional and purposeful recruitment of a technical specialist (the French colleague with many years of experience) and a range of allies (employees, farmers, and suppliers) helped her navigate the difficult terrain of cultural, financial, and structural challenges in Burkina Faso. She motivated and enabled employees to directly and actively engage in the fight to save the company and she got them to stand side-by-side with her. Both the technical specialist and her allies provided valuable advice, counsel, and solutions as she navigated the turnaround.

Sometimes, though, it isn't the advisers, coaches or allies that help you to grow, or even just to get through. It's your determination. Your vision. Your resilience. Your courage. Yourself.

The leadership journey of Anne-Sophie d'Andlau and her partner Catherine Berjal has not been easy, but they stayed the course powered by their vision and conviction that what they were doing was important and meaningful. They faced opposition professionally and personally. Professionally, because their business idea was revolutionary. Personally, because they were two women in a male-dominated industry.

'It has not been easy,' d'Andlau says, 'but we had a vision to create something different in the investment space and that vision kept us going. Even during very difficult times, our joint vision kept us moving forward.'

Ten years ago, they set out to develop a way of managing funds that produced not only financial performance, but also addressed environmental, social and governance (ESG) matters.

'People in the industry thought it is not necessary to tackle all those issues of governance, environment, social,' she says. 'They were not sure if we could really deliver value.'

But they proved with their performance that they could.

'And our activism is pretty vocal. We don't like to be in public space much, that is not our personalities. But we didn't have any choice – we had to confront boards that operated behind closed doors in the public space. Now it doesn't matter, because we created a very strong brand

and we can have very interesting discussions behind the closed doors, we don't need to go public so much.'

Although some people might worry about constant confrontations as a way forward, d'Andlau is positive.

'After 10 years of fighting battles, creating the kind of investment firm we envisioned, our original vision and purpose hasn't changed at all. We are pushing for better governance and create some sort of counter power within this very clubby male environment in Europe and open up opportunities for more diversity and benefit to the environment.'

Anne-Sophie d'Andlau has extensive experience of the drawbacks of the clubby male environment.

'I started my leadership journey in Paris in corporate finance,' she says. 'I quickly realized, as a woman, I was in a minority and could not really relate to the work environment. I remember I had just started and the partners wanted to invite me for lunch to welcome me. And during lunch, they kept on talking about girls, women, and made jokes like in a super-French way. I thought to myself, "You can't do that. On what planet are you living?"'

But she didn't shy away from the task. In fact, she tackled tougher projects in her next role.

D'Andlau was asked to participate in the launch of the first hedge fund in France and she accepted it.

'In the hedge fund world, being a woman is an uphill battle most of the time. I found myself as the only woman in the trading room with 20+ men. I felt the minority stuff big time. I found it very difficult. I struggled the first six months, it was really tough, but I fought.'

What made it difficult?

'It was a super-male culture: going to clubs, bottles of champagne, and all sorts of different situations. I didn't feel I was part of that culture, I was just doing my job and working really hard. I continued to fight all battles and had two kids in the meantime.'

After her first child, she felt pressure to return to work as soon as she could.

'After my first child, I came back to work immediately to defend my position – there were many men who were ready to take over. I took more time with my second child, but I never gave up the battle.'

Eventually the hedge fund was bought by a bank and she decided to leave. That's also the time when she met her partner Catherine Berjal, who was also ready to quit her position, and they decided to launch their own investment firm.

'IT WAS LIKE JUMPING IN A COLD BATH'

The first barriers to overcome were the regulations and seed investment. 'It was like jumping in a cold bath,' she says. 'It took us 15 months before we were able to launch our first fund.'

She thinks back for a moment.

'Yes, it was a rough process.'

After three years, they parted ways with their investor because of significant differences. 'So we started back to zero,' she says.

They kept going, however. Picking themselves up. Relying on each other for support.

'Today, after seven years, we are on our own, without big institutions holding us back. We are able to express ourselves and deliver really good performance and grow the funds and become who we are today.'

It's not only entrepreneurs like d'Andlau who face professional and personal obstacles in their leadership journey. Andrea Buetler, originally from Switzerland, has spent most of her working life in Laos, Hong Kong, and Singapore with companies including Atkins, Advision, and Worley. At first it was a culture shock, but when she opened herself to the local culture, she found she developed as a leader.

Now Director of Energy Transition for the Asia Pacific region for Worley, based in Singapore, she recalls how disoriented she felt at first. 'My first really challenging leadership position was when I decided to take a job in Laos in my late 20s,' she says.

She was inspired to do something very different from what was possible in Switzerland. 'I took a role as the Head of Sales and Marketing for a medium-sized enterprise based in Laos called Sunlabob Renewable Energy, managing five to seven people, reporting directly to the CEO.'

She had never met the CEO or the rest of the team. 'I had the boldness, in a way, just to go and try it.'

Her responsibilities included acquiring new clients, supporting the delivery processes, and developing strategy for the company. 'The challenges were very large and difficult,' she says. 'When I got there, it was really tough. However, looking back it is also one of those places where

I personally grew the most.'

The challenges she faced included the language barrier, the industry, and the culture. 'Managing people which are from a completely different cultural background and with only broken English skills was really hard for me,' she says. 'Then also the market was so new for me. The type of business was new for me.'

Had she underestimated the challenges of living in a completely new culture?

'I think I had underestimated the challenges. I had to figure out the most basic things to survive personally. What can I have for breakfast? How can I get around? It wasn't like in Switzerland, you can just ride your bike everywhere. Everything was different.'

Like other next-generation leaders, she coped by focusing on her purpose – the reason why she was there. 'I soon realized that not only I had huge business responsibility, but also a social responsibility,' she says.

The business was a social enterprise. It had to hire and retain people from less fortunate backgrounds. If Buetler couldn't retain them, it would be difficult for them to get another job and to feed their families.

'It is one of the times in my life that I've worked the hardest and longest hours. And had the most pressure, both business pressure and social responsibility pressure. I was working to the point of exhaustion.'

GETTING IN TOUCH WITH LOCAL CULTURES

On the other hand, this was when she began to open herself to the local culture. 'I was learning to tune into Laos where there are many temples, monks, and everything is very slow. It was two extremes. In the office, I had extreme high pressure. When I walked out of the office, everything was calm and you can hear monks chanting in the temples.'

Buetler managed to balance the pressures of work with the pressures of just living. 'I learned to meditate, enjoy walks in nature. And participated in social time with my colleagues and learned about their culture.'

What would that have been like in a big city?

'If I was doing that role in New York, let's say, I would have definitely been burned-out. Even today I draw from my time in Laos. Whenever I have these phases I am really stressed, I try to remind myself – hey, what did I do back in Laos?'

The kind of self-transformation that Buetler experienced is something today's leaders are acutely aware of.

Debbie O'Neill learned the hard way that being a good leader, especially in a fast-paced start-up setting, requires self-awareness and recognition of the signs of emotional, mental, and physical exhaustion caused by excessive and prolonged stress.

Now the VP, Domestic Partnerships, at US online shopping platform Honey, she was one of the first three employees at a mobile advertising company.

'I was hired as a sales representative,' she says. 'However, as we started to grow, I was doing everything – hiring, onboarding, coaching, managing, even furnishing the office.'

O'Neill found herself building desks and chairs with the others as they hired people.

'We were our own finance people. We were our own operations. We were our own lawyers. We were the salespeople. We were the account management. We became very well rounded in running the business. We were hiring people right out of college, 21 years old, kids who need coaching and mentoring. Naturally, everybody starting looking at me for guidance.'

As well as being a salesperson, O'Neill was simultaneously taking on a leadership role – a situation she describes as 'playing both sides of the coin'.

'I was an aggressive seller and doing very well and aggressively hiring, teaching, and leading the team,' she says.

'From there I went up the leadership ladder quickly, still selling aggressively and leading the organization and the teams. Still playing both sides of the coin, which was really hard actually.'

What was particularly hard?

'I think sometimes I forgot about myself and would give 100 per cent to the people and give 100 per cent to the clients. At some point I kind of lost myself.'

She thought she was simply practicing the work ethic instilled in her by her family. 'I had grown up in Ireland, working in our family bar and restaurant. Everybody in my family very much put their heads down and worked. I thought I was practicing that good work ethic. In reality, I had burned out, and my body could not take it anymore.'

Yet O'Neill was very successful and was making a good deal of money.

'But I wish somebody had told me to slow down. I had completely burned out, stressed out, and I was diagnosed with an ulcer. My hair was falling out.'

Burn-out is not good for team members or the business, let alone the individual concerned. 'I learned the hard way that a good leader should be able to set limits for themselves and for their teams and say, "Put your computer away. Don't work weekends. Don't work late into the night."'

Something had to give, she knew. 'I had to change myself and learn to bring more balance into my life.'

But changing yourself is not easy. 'It took some time for me to admit I messed up and show humility and admit that I am not perfect. Even as a leader you mess up. I learned to humanize my mistakes and found that people started to relate to me and trust me even more. People felt, "Oh, I don't feel afraid to go to her when I mess up, because I am human and we can all make mistakes".'

In the same way Adrian Locher took a sabbatical to work out what he wanted to do with his life, O'Neill had to step back, taking a break for even a few hours, as the best way to figure out what sort of leader she wanted to be.

One of the big challenges facing Tara Hovey at her family's construction business Optima was managing the leadership succession. She knew she had to look after herself to look after the business, but she also felt she needed a break to transform herself as a leader.

'Leading a high-risk, high-stress construction business and negotiating big deals and managing the leadership succession in my family was a very challenging time,' she says.

'Being thoughtful about navigating a smooth succession was hard work because it was all about emotions.

'My family was not particularly good about talking about emotions. I had to really lead these conversations and actually bring everybody together and talk about the business thing and the underlying emotions beneath it. How we are feeling? How we are working together? What roles are each of us playing?'

How did she handle this time?

'There is no way I could have led through that period of time without meditation practice. Given my work schedule, I had to focus all my time outside of work environment on kind of self-recovery downtime. Just to get clarity on the issues so I was not coming from a place of reactivity or lack of focus, I had to use all the tools I know, like fitness, meditation, yoga, and mindfulness. I could not have continued through some of those challenges and stresses, ups-and-downs, without all these tools.'

Even with all the coping strategies in place, could she keep it up?

'It was not sustainable. I finally came to a realization that I had to take a step back, take a sabbatical and come back as a leader and with a leadership style that is much more sustainable for my life. Even though I had these great tools that helped me power through, I was still draining myself everyday more than filling myself.'

A BURNED-OUT LEADER IS NO GOOD TO ANYONE

Hovey learned, as O'Neill learned, that a burned-out leader is no good to anyone.

'A big part of this sabbatical is coming back home to myself and reflecting on the last few years,' says Hovey. 'I am taking radical self-responsibility for everything in my life: the struggles, challenges, the burnout, traumatic things. I am taking radical self-responsibility for everything and it is also empowering.'

What has she learned?

'I could see that I had a choice and there were many times where I was just putting everyone else's needs ahead of mine – my company, my executive team, my family – to the point where I realized I had to fulfill myself before I could keep giving.'

Kevin Jolly, Head of Business Analytics at TIER Mobility, the urban mobility company based in Berlin, Germany, also practices mindfulness to improve his leadership interactions.

'If your mind fluctuates and you are agitated, I believe that your team can sense it,' he says. 'They feel that you are not someone who can lead with confidence. They feel that you are someone who is anxious and shaky. It is very important to me that I don't come across that way.'

He has two pieces of advice for younger professionals. 'Number one, don't work until 2am in the morning, no matter how much your manager tells you to change the presentation deck. You really have to develop time management skills so you can take control of your life.'

And number two?

'Number two, realize early that life is way more than work and always stay grounded and be humble in reality. No matter how high you get in life, it's not about yourself. It's definitely about staying in a very neutral state of mind and using that mind to specifically help people at specific times in your life.'

Finding that balance between work and life is part of being a good leader, as Adrian Locher of Merantix discovered to his cost. 'Despite being a successful entrepreneur and building and selling companies, I started to learn a lot about myself when I crashed my private life,' he says.

'I got divorced, very recently, but it was a long process. The breakdown happened two to three years ago. That really forced me to come to a halt and look at things a bit more thoroughly and closer, and I also learned a lot about myself. That was most surely the most difficult time of my life.'

As with O'Neill and Hovey, Locher has learned that he needs to take care of himself.

'I started to work my way out of pain. I had tried a lot of the tools and methods, and one theme that worked super-well on me was meditation. I learned to slow down a little bit and pay attention to not only what, but how, we're doing things. I found that really interesting.'

What else helped?

'Another tool was reading philosophy. It helped me change my focus a bit. I realized there are actually three buckets that are important to me. First, family. Second, business. And third is myself.'

It's been a fascinating part of my research for this book to see people realize that personal growth and self-care are just as important as business growth and caring for your team..

'For me now,' says Locher, 'if there is a certain balance in these three areas, life is good for me. I learned to invest more time in myself and spend more time with myself.'

There are no short-cuts, Locher says.

'You cannot simply optimize one single dimension because the system will ultimately break. For me, it was to focus more on mindfulness and self-knowledge. I also realized a very essential truth – you can only be a good leader if you know yourself.'

If you know yourself, only then can you hope to help your team to grow. And that's a whole other ball game. ■

“I am very much under pressure to deliver against my targets and recover my full cost, deliver operational excellence, so on… While I am doing all that, I keep reminding myself not to forget about the people, about the team, about creating an environment where they can be elevated and happy.

Catherine Li
CEO, Asia Pacific
Atkins

Chapter 7

TEAMS ARE THE HEARTBEAT OF THE COMPANY

How the New Leaders of Change unleash the potential of teams

It doesn't seem so long ago. 'I can remember the sheer joy of competition, hard work, and passion leading a high-performing sales team in my early 20s,' says Catherine Li of her time working for a Hong Kong investment company.

'We were about 10 people, all young, fresh out of college,' she says. 'I remember the feeling of helping each other to succeed and wanting to be the best performing team in the firm.'

Li is now CEO for Asia Pacific for Atkins, the design and engineering consultancy, and her words epitomize what the next generation of leaders get out of leading a team.

'The company culture was competitive,' she says, 'but the competition was between teams – there were about 10 teams and we were all competing with each other.'

This culture encouraged her team to try to be the best. 'As the team leader, I was always thinking, how do I create a high-performing team? How do we win?'

She also learned, as a leader, that personal performance is important too. 'I had to act as a leader role model and gain technical credibility. So I became the highest performing sales manager and my team was the highest performing team.'

Building a great team is both art and science. 'I remember just a sense of mission, sense of achievement and success, and collectively how we influence each other as well,' says Li. 'After so many years, I still think about that experience, that feeling of accomplishment, teamwork, and energy. It is hard to replicate, but the feeling has stayed with me all these years.'

Li's exhilarating experience as the team leader of a high-performing team underlines the two important elements that make a great team. The team members have to understand that they are interdependent and need each other for success ('helping each other to succeed'), and the team leader needs to be authentic and competent ('I became the highest performing sales manager'). If as a leader, you can't motivate your team to collaborate and you are not competent, you will not get the buy-in, and you won't cultivate high-performing teamwork.

The next generation of leaders understand this. It doesn't mean they are not worried about making profits – just that they want more from, and for, their teams.

But there are many types of teams, each with different purpose, membership, and outcomes. And the nature of teams and their work is evolving, as leaders, organizations, and institutions change the way they are structured, governed, and led.

As the organizational models move away from siloed functional hierarchies, top-down leadership, and bureaucratic practices, we need a seismic shift in how we define, lead, and construct teams. In addition, today's complex challenges require teams to operate in an ambiguous and rapidly changing environment. Successful teams need to embrace a new way of working – one that harnesses the power of collaboration, diverse perspectives, iterative experimentation, and creative thinking.

So in today's social, economic, and global context, what should high-performing team leaders do differently?

Project Aristotle, a Google research program, highlights five factors that make a team successful[28]:

- having structured and clear roles and goals,
- having dependable team members,
- doing work that has meaning or purpose,
- doing work that impacts the company and customers,
- and ensuring psychological safety within the team.

This last point – creating psychological safety – is the factor that stands out for me in the context of leading change in the 21st century.[29] Because to create psychological safety, team members must be comfortable in taking risks, promoting their ideas, and communicating their feelings.

So what behaviors promote psychological safety in teams? Well, as Google discovered, it is the team's traditions, its rituals, its behavioral standards – the unwritten rules around how team members treat each other – that are essential to its success and performance. Leaders have a significant influence on these cultural norms and behaviors. But it can be a difficult thing to get to grips with.

'Changing corporate culture can be extremely complicated and at first you have to really understand and learn the rules of competitive behaviors that underpin corporate cultures,' says Fonta Hadley, behavioral researcher, listening teacher and the founder of Eloquence, a communication training studio in San Francisco, USA.

Unfortunately, for many executives those rules are based on the wrong thing, she says. 'It is not a game of people,' she says. 'It's a game of winning. But what's fascinating about that is that it actually is the game of people at the end.'

She pauses to think about what she's just said.

'It's ironic, right? To win, you need to work through your people and with your people.'

Healthy forms of competition and a drive to win can be fun in and between teams. I think most of us have enjoyed fun competitions and games at work. It can boost motivation, effort, and performance. Competition becomes toxic, however, when it loses the fun aspect and becomes a zero-sum game where it becomes more about 'they failed, I won'. This mindset forges disruptive behaviors such as reluctance to share information, working in isolation, fear of failure, and constantly needing to prove your worth and defend your merits.

There's a fine line between healthy and toxic team competition. And it can be crossed very quickly, sometimes without any awareness.

'I think when you are invested in winning at all costs, you not only act inhumanely towards others, but also towards yourself,' says Hadley. 'The competition and the belief that "I must win" is pulling you away from yourself.'

She is very concerned about the wellbeing of the executives she works with. 'These young founders who walk into my office and all I can say is, "Oh my God, you look like hell!" They have dark circles under their eyes. They are either overweight or really thin. They can't sit still. They are constantly pulsing and ticking. They behave like they are being chased by something really scary.'

She says this is why people are looking for an alternative. They are drawn to the concepts of emotional intelligence, mindfulness, empathy, and vulnerability. 'It is because we are looking for alternative ways to work and treat each other and break free of the winning, competition, and narcissistic mindset.'

Leaders who are skilled at empathetic collaboration ask questions instead of calling shots, actively listening, assuming a curious mindset, and building on others' ideas.

'Millennial leaders are transforming leadership,' says Banks Baker, Head of Global Partnerships at Google, 'by dismantling hierarchical organizational structures and leading with values like transparency, humility, and growth mindset.'

He describes this relationship between leader and team as stewardship, which he believes benefits the business as well as employees. 'As I started to look at how I was building teams and leading, this concept of stewardship versus ownership started to emerge.'[30]

What does that mean in essence?

'I don't see myself as an employee at Google,' says Baker. 'I see Google as my client. The stewardship framework helps me make better decisions because I'm not compromised by trying to sustain my position. I am there to create forward momentum for the business. I'm there to ensure that the best future-looking path is being considered and that I'm not making unnatural decisions to consolidate my power or to fortify my role or to sustain my financial gain.'

So when you see yourself as an employee, you become compromised? 'Exactly,' he says.

'If I look at it as stewardship and I look at it through a lens of service, then I start making better decisions. And I think that works in the business side, but I think it also really works on the team side.'

For example, Baker shares his values with team members when they come on board. 'I have this conversation with everybody that joins my team and I bring up the concept of stewardship versus ownership. I say, listen, I don't own you. You're not my asset. And so, yes, you might be in my reporting line, but I am a steward and you are in my care.'

Baker sees his role as developing his team member. 'My role is to grow you,' he says 'and make you more and more efficient and make you more and more successful and ensure that you're going in the direction you need.'

AN UNEXPECTED SIGN OF STRENGTH

Old-style leaders might be uncomfortable with this way of working, regarding this idea of service and stewardship as a sign of weakness. Not Baker. 'I believe there is nothing wrong and weak about you being here to serve,' he says. 'It's about seeing your role both as a business and as a leader, as truly being here to serve, serve your communities, serve your employees, serve your customers, and do it in a way that is truly heartfelt and centered around them.'

He's very clear on this and he emphasizes the fact. 'I don't think there's a weakness in that. I think that there's incredible value and it's an incredibly noble thing to spend your short period here on the planet to do.'

It's all about ensuring the team members can work independently, he says, which keeps the whole team and ultimately the whole business agile, too.

While what Google does to build teams is worth studying, early-stage start-up teams more naturally behave in an agile and adaptive way and can be even better examples to learn from.

Wunderflats, for example, is a German marketplace for temporary, furnished housing. When its founders set it up, they knew they needed a multi-functional team, but they had no formal requirements for hiring people.

'We just knew we needed marketing, developers, salespeople,' says Jan Hase, co-founder and CEO. 'We conducted interviews over a coffee in cafés, in a very relaxed atmosphere. We did know that we wanted smart, creative, and get-things-done type of people – and no assholes!'

Hase worked from the back of a café and went bar hopping every Wednesday evening to find team members. Why?

'Those informal social interactions provided a space for us to get to know each other in a more personal way, a more humane way, and build trust relationships. It took us four weeks to raise the first round of funding and we hired the first 10 employees then. We didn't have a long-term plan, but we had a really strong belief in the vision of what Wunderflats could be.'

Hase has a strange vision for how they were operating at the time of the launch.

'We were operating like pirates, we were doing everything unconventionally. We focused on what needed to get done and we all contributed. We didn't think about roles or we didn't have mental models of how to do stuff. We just did it. There was so much stuff to do. And people were switching from being a developer to being a salesperson. We were constantly talking to each other, solving problems, and knew what everyone was doing.'

Soon Wunderflats grew from 10 people to 20, to 50, to 80 and now 120. 'We are moving through different stages really fast,' says Hase.

BEYOND A 'FAMILY' BUSINESS

As it grew, Hase learned he could no longer know everything about everyone. 'It was when we were 20, I realized things were changing. I still talked to everyone, but I didn't know what they were doing day-to-day.'

There is a sense of sadness in what he says.

'When we were 50 or more, I had to let go and accept that it was not like a family business anymore. We eventually moved into an office space and had more of an organizational structure, even though it was flat and very dynamic.'

Finding the right people for your teams – the ones who will make your purpose live – is key, says Adrian Locher of Merantix Venture Studio. 'After several start-ups, my key learning actually has become an obsession: I am obsessed with creating the right purpose-driven culture, with the right set of values, and hiring the right people.'

It takes some humility as a leader to give decision-making power to other people, even though it means there will be times he does not agree with the decision. And sometimes their decision may lead to not such a good outcome. But he's cool with that.

'I hire someone to my team because I believe she or he is much better at their role than I am, so they have the decision power in their area and you have to let them take risks, experiment, and learn from their mistakes.'

Should there be mistakes? Should he allow this?

'There will be mistakes and you cannot go and take the decision power back and manage it yourself. Not if you want to build a scalable leadership model. If you do that you are going to be a dictator and everything will be going through yourself and that is not a scalable system. I would rather prefer to enable this person. Mistakes are part of the game of learning, that is how you learn. I focus on creating a risk- and failure-tolerating culture.'

If leaders are going to take such a mature position, and delegate decision-making responsibility, the key reassurance is to know you've brought in the right people.

And the new generation of leaders in my study, regardless of whether they are working in a start-up or a traditional company, seem to believe that the best way to achieve this is to build a team focused on interpersonal relationships. Of course, the team needs a clear purpose and mission, but the individual team members are hired not only for their technical fit, but also – and more importantly – for their cultural fit.

When the new generation of leaders try to find top performers, they pay special attention to emotional intelligence and cultural fit. For them, the technical skills and IQ are important threshold competencies. They are needed to get the job done. However, the magic competencies are related to how much emotional intelligence (EQ) the candidate is able to demonstrate.

The skills that make up EQ were summarized by former journalist Daniel Goleman at his best in *Working with Emotional Intelligence* (1999):

- self-awareness of your emotional state,
- self-regulation of your emotions,
- empathy – the ability to put yourself in other people's shoes,
- social skills around communication, negotiation, conflict resolution, and the recognition and praise of others' achievements.

Importantly, the World Economic Forum agrees with the new generation of leaders on the value of hiring for EQ.[31] 'Overall, social skills – such as persuasion, emotional intelligence and teaching others – will be in higher demand across industries than narrow technical skills, such as programming or equipment operation and control,' it says. 'In essence, technical skills will need to be supplemented with strong social and collaboration skills.'

Adrian Locher is well aware of the importance of hiring people with the right combination of skills. He leads a portfolio of start-up companies and in all of them they focus on both intelligence and emotional intelligence. 'We don't compromise and we weigh both factors 50/50,' he says.

'We would never a hire a person because she or he is amazingly skilled and smart technically. There has to be a cultural and social fit with the team. I try to hire the smartest and the nicest people who also have a massive potential and eagerness to be developed. This is the core foundation of how I build companies today.'

The ability to establish trust rapidly with new team members requires personal and interpersonal awareness, empathy, and genuine interest from the leaders, too – something this new generation of leaders seem to have in common.

WHEN HIRING FAILS, ACT FAST

Of course, hiring people doesn't always work out. 'No matter how robust the hiring system you have, there are times something slips and you end up hiring the wrong person,' says Locher. 'When that happens, you have to act really fast and let that person go.'

What was his biggest mistake in this area?

'The single biggest mistake I did in the past was, I hired too fast and fired too slow, which is something I try to change every day.'

There's something else on his mind, though, and it's equally as important as his hiring strategy. For a start-up, the team, he believes, is even more important than the idea.

'If you want to build an amazing company, it doesn't really matter with what idea you start. It doesn't really matter what kind of market you start. But if you start with the right team, ultimately the company is going to be successful because a great team will always find its way around obstacles and make things successful.'

And building great teams inevitably leads to other things. 'That is the one single most important factor in building great companies – building, assembling, and developing great teams.'

Catherine Li of Atkins agrees about the importance of finding the right people – and the importance of acting decisively when something isn't right.

'My last role as the Managing Director and current role as the CEO for the Asia Pacific region taught me a great deal about people and how to develop high-performing teams,' she says.

'I really think the biggest learning for me was people – how do you put the right people in the right roles, and the right teams?'

What happens when you inherit someone else's team as a leader? What then?

'I had to redesign the team I inherited, I brought in some new people. And I had to let go of a few senior people as well, who were not a good fit and were not performing at the level I expected. I was also really surprised at how a couple of people I promoted performed at such high levels.'

The difference in their performance was amazing, she says, and not at all what she was expecting. 'It was a great lesson in the importance of identifying the right talent and understanding what they can and want to do best, and then giving them a platform and supporting them to deliver. It was very powerful to watch that happen.'

What about those who don't work out for you?

'Actually you need to be decisive about letting go of people who are not a good fit. I kept coming back to the team culture I wanted to create. Because for me it is about having a high-performing team in a high-performing team culture. If you're not part of the team, if you don't care about your team members, if you don't trust and respect your team members, I don't have a space for you.'

For Li this even applies for senior people.

'I had to let go a couple of quite senior level leaders who were my direct line reports. I also wanted to show and be a role model to others on the team that I don't tolerate people who are not team players.'

After a time as Managing Director, she has now been in the CEO role for six months. How is that different?

'It is much more complicated, both from business and organizational management level,' she says. 'For example, I spend more time dealing with corporate leaders and corporate reports than my own team at times. But I am much more clear that my role is all about people, other people, versus myself. My biggest vision as a leader is, how can I make people who work for me happy?'

Does that mean she lets the numbers slide?

'Don't get me wrong, I am very much under pressure to deliver against my targets and recover my full cost, deliver operational excellence, so on. While I am doing all that, I keep reminding myself not to forget about the people, about the team, about creating an environment where they can be elevated and happy. Because Atkins is in a people business, we are a professional services company with consultants and engineers.'

There's one word that Li continues to use and it seems odd for such a senior business executive.

'If I had to pick one word for everything it has to be "happiness". How can I create a culture where people feel happy at work? I know that is going to influence the business and clients. If you show up positive, upbeat, ambitious, and happy, the clients are going to feel that and they are going to want to work with you.'

Unfortunately, some people are not happy – and one person's unhappiness can harm the whole team. As Donna See, CEO of Xora Innovation, discovered, it's important to act properly and quickly in this case.

She was managing a team of 30 as the director of a healthcare program, partnering with all of the major healthcare institutions in New York City, both public and private, inpatient and outpatient, to improve the childhood immunization rate. This was a big issue at that time in New York because of a number of polio and measles outbreaks.

'The team I put together was extremely passionate and excited about our mission,' she says. 'We were given funding to design and renovate our own building and that experience made us even closer. We were a very tight team. There was a lot of passion and energy for what we were doing.'

However, one member of the team didn't seem to belong. 'Over time I became aware of a team member who was extremely disruptive,' See says. 'Other people on the team had come to me and said, this person's bringing down the team camaraderie and constantly complaining about everything. I made the decision to ask him to leave quite quickly – and that was a big decision for me because I had never fired anybody before.'

How did that feel?

'I remember being overwhelmed with the decision because his performance was okay, he was actually doing a good job, but he was extremely disruptive to the team, and team members were suffering. I tried to coach him and say, "Listen, here are the issues." But for whatever reason it wasn't sinking in and so then I had to make a call.'

What did you take from this?

'What I learned from that story is that once you have built a very tight team and a certain culture, it is very important to protect that – to protect the culture we created to achieve what we want to achieve.'

The fascinating aspect of this is that she had not learned this from a previous role. She was really reacting just from pure instinct, she says.

LEARN TO BE INTENTIONAL

'Now I think about things like this very intentionally. I go out of my way to make certain decisions, put in place certain practices and use certain language when we talk about things, how we approach things. I want to build a culture of trust, very intentionally and purposefully.'

As See discovered, one employee's disruptive behavior can affect the performance of an entire team. And because the New Leaders of Change put a high value on creating a supportive, collaborative, trusting team culture, they cannot tolerate members who are disruptive or who erode the quality of colleague relationships.

To be fair, team performance, motivation, and adaptability is a complex interplay between the individual, the team as a whole, the style of the leader, other internal and external influences, and the team environment. But when there's conflict the key thing the New Leaders of Change have learned is not to ignore it.

Luckily there's a growing body of research showing how devastating even a single disruptive team member can be to team morale, engagement, productivity, employee retention, and profitability. One classic study of 800 managers and employees reported in *Harvard Business Review* found data that's well worth reflecting on.[32]

- 80 per cent of employees lost work time worrying about a single disruptive employee's rude behavior;

- 78 per cent said their commitment to the organization declined in the face of toxic behavior;
- 66 per cent said their performance declined;
- 63 per cent lost work time in avoiding the individual;
- 38 per cent 'intentionally decreased' the quality of their work;
- 25 per cent of employees who had been treated rudely admitted taking their frustrations out on customers;
- 12 per cent left their jobs due to team culture created by the disruptive employee.

So it's no wonder that many of the leaders I spoke with struggled to articulate exactly what it is that inspires and motivates their teams to perform. However, they all intuitively understand that they need to consciously design and develop their teams and the culture they hope for. That they need to establish meaningful relationships with the individuals in their teams. That they need to be aware of their leadership influence on their teams. And that they need to be aware of, and respond to, the things that influence the motivation and performance of their teams.

It's easy to see that the new generation of leaders put care and relationships at the heart of their approach to building high-performance teams.

Traditional-style leaders may balk at this. 'Care in business? Why in a business context would we need to mention care?'

But as far as the next generation of leaders is concerned, it's essential. They value – and demonstrate – taking care of team members' well-being in personal and professional situations. The leaders in my study firmly believe it to be a significant factor in their leadership success.

'I get really interested in my team members and try to understand who they are, what they are struggling with, and what makes them passionate,' says Donna See.

'One of my team members was diagnosed with a rare cancer while she was going through a divorce. I basically covered for her because she ran out of her disability insurance and I wanted to extend the loyalty. It was my personal contribution to her wellbeing. I listened to my gut and wanted to do the right thing in this situation.'

What happened next?

'We are very close even today, even though, on the business side, we actually have been on opposite sides of the table several times since then.'

It was tough, but she wouldn't change anything, she says. She would not want to work in a company where this caring relationship wasn't possible. 'I don't know if my leadership style would work in very large organizations where I didn't have a direct contact, relationship, with the people. I've always been in a skunkworks-type of situation with mission-oriented teams – that's what I have sought out in terms of my career.'

Google's Aman Narain, Global New Payments Ecosystems Lead in Singapore, has a similar story about a former team member. 'I value building relationships with my team members and ensuring that they understand that, even though I am demanding, I care about them.'

I ask if this has any real impact and, if so, how does he know?

'I continually get emails from my previous team members who just want to keep in touch or update me on how they are doing. For example, a couple days ago I got an email from a previous team member who wanted to say thank you. She informed me that she is doing really well and she wanted to thank me because I helped her during a tough spot in her life.'

This was a young Indian woman working in the team as a junior analyst. She had come to Singapore through an arranged marriage. 'She came to me one day asking for advice and literally broke down – her husband had left her and she had no money.' She was being forced to leave Singapore and go back to her family in India.

'I gave her a spot bonus and provided her with the coaching and counseling she needed. I said, "Take the money, get legal help and don't leave Singapore and you are going to be great."'

And now? 'Now she is doing fantastic.'

Some commentators might wonder if supporting individuals really matters. How does it help the team?

The New Leaders of Change believe that if you help people achieve their personal goals, you also help the team – and therefore the company.

'As a leader, when you can help align team and business goals with the people's individual goals, they are super-excited to be there. They work really hard,' says Banks Baker of Google.

He lets his team members know he cares about their personal aspirations. 'I don't want people that just want to work on my team because they want a job,' he says. 'I don't think anybody wants someone in their team who says: "I just needed a job and I got this one." I don't think it is good for them, I don't think it is good for the team, and I don't think it's good for the business.'

What advice does he give to new leaders to pave the way for this?

'I would rather start very early in our relationship to have deep conversations about what is it that they want to achieve, what are their personal vision and aspirations, what do they want to get out their experience in Google.'

He gives this example, when he's talking to a new team member, saying, 'Google has certain things that it wants to get out of you. And those are pretty clear – they're in your job description and they're in the mission and the strategy of the team. But my hope is you have something personal you want to get out of this. My hope is it's something deeper than just some money, because if you just want money, I could probably recommend some other places to work.'

Baker is clear on this.

'If you have longer-term career aspirations or personal aspirations, I need to know those and I will help you get there. I will support you if you want to be here eight years or 24 months.'

Then he works with them to identify what their end destination is and what key skills they will need – and even when will be a good time for them to leave.

'I look at some of the best relationships I have with team members and they're with people who've left,' he says. 'I had one team member, a Brazilian woman, who used to work for the United Nations. She was involved with indigenous people's rights in Brazil. Then she joined my team. As I got to know her, I realized that she probably had a short lifecycle at Google. Her personal aspiration was that she wanted to go back to Brazil, and continue to focus on indigenous people's rights there.'

So what did he do?

'Together we identified the skills she could develop at her role in my team at Google. We agreed that to run a non-profit focused on indigenous people's rights she needed to develop how to build large-scale partnerships, complex negotiations, contracts, and conflict management skills. And she would then be able to go back into an NGO with a very sharp set of skills that could be utilized to make her more successful than she was in the past.'

So the two of them focused on specific projects that enabled her to develop those skills. They put her into some really complex negotiations. They put her in front of some very complex partner relationships. They put her in front of big programs that required cross-functional collaboration, across many teams. That way she could learn about aligning incentives and finding consensus.

'Ultimately, she was benefiting Google and adding value to Google at every step of the way while she was developing skills to make her successful in her future vision.'

When this team member left the US, she returned to work in the Amazon where she has started a nonprofit, is on the board of another nonprofit, and is focusing on the preservation of indigenous people, their lands and cultures.

When you can align employees' personal goals with the business goals, Baker says, you will 'get people to work really, really hard, and they're super-excited to be there. And you don't have people that are just wallowing in negativity. You don't have people that feel like they're just putting in some time, but they don't know what they're going to do with their lives. Then they get aggravated and they get frustrated and they get demoralized.'

He pauses for a second to sum things up for me.

'I'd rather have super-excited people here for 12 months and start over than have any of that aggravation and frustration.'

Banks Baker, Donna See, and Aman Narain are among a new cadre of leaders who have deep awareness of their team members' personal challenges (demonstrating empathy), and take action to help them in a very practical way (demonstrating compassion).

Empathy and compassion might not be the qualities you think of when considering what it takes to succeed as a leader and build high-performing teams. However, according to Worline and Dutton (2017) there is increasing research evidence to show that empathy and compassion in the workplace are related to positive outcomes such as improved employee wellbeing, improved customer and employee engagement, increased productivity, creativity, innovation, adaptability to change, and reduced cost to the business.

FROM EMPATHY AND COMPASSION TO MISSION AND PURPOSE

With the Covid-19 pandemic and the rapid acceptance of hybrid working practices, after decades when the HR movement has tried and failed to add working from home to the agenda, you begin to wonder if organizations finally are being compassionate and leading with empathy during these trying times. Will the same now be true, I wonder, when it comes to leading with purpose?

Leah Belsky, Chief Enterprise Officer at Coursera, an online learning provider, puts it well. 'For me, it's always been about aligning the team on the team purpose, with a mission and clear goals – having an aligned mission and shared goals that everyone's on the same page about – and then supporting the team to achieve those goals.'

When everyone understands the purpose, Belsky trusts the team members to work out how to achieve the goals. 'Once we are aligned on goals, as leader I support my team by giving them a lot of space and allow them the creativity and freedom to achieve those goals. If things in the schedule or cost shift, of course I will come back to the goals and review with the team. How are we tracking against our goals? How are we not tracking?'

But once again the start point is recruitment.

'My approach tends to be hire really talented, smart, and passionate people, create close alignment and give them a lot space to get it done. Also, making the whole experience not about me but about the leadership team as a whole. We invest a lot in the team and relationships between the team members. So the team can learn from many different places, from each other, not necessarily from me.'

It's worth taking time, she believes, to achieve this clarity of mission. 'Where I've found the most success,' she says, 'is when I am able to build a strong team culture around a clear mission, why you are doing what you are doing. That clarity of an aligned and meaningful mission feels like a start-up within a start-up, whether it is a functional team or business team. It creates a huge excitement around the mission, driving goals, and expanding.

'My advice to the younger generation of leaders is, be clear about the type of problems and challenges that you want to solve in the world and make sure those are aligned both with your passions as well as career opportunities that exists. And then from there, it's a matter of surrounding yourself with people who also want to take on similar challenges.'

That's where it starts, she says, and that is the root of great leadership. 'It's about creating and building together. If you're aligned around shared mission, goals, and passions and you root your leadership in that, then a lot of the rest becomes about kind of tactics and practices.'

And on this subject of tactics and practices, in all the interviews I have conducted, there is a common thread. No one I've talked to believes that team motivation and empowerment depend on gimmicky things like installing ping-pong tables or organizing bring-your-dog-to-work days. They believe it's more fundamental than that. It depends on the need all human beings have to search for and find meaning and a purpose in life.

And by purpose, they do not mean a vague vision, mission or values statement lying dormant in some PowerPoint deck. They mean a purpose that taps into people's desire for meaning. Something that ignites their passion and inspires them.

Of course, making people feel psychologically safe requires great emotional intelligence. And most of the next generation of leaders I've spoken to think this is a vital quality in a good leader. But also, they say, it's needed in their team members.

Team members who have a high degree of self-awareness are better able to handle interactions with other team members in situations that require empathy and understanding. They know their own strengths and weaknesses, which means that they are more likely to say when they don't know something, or when they need assistance from someone else on the team. They have self-confidence, which means they are comfortable with experimenting and not feeling that a failed experiment reflects poorly on their abilities.

People with high emotional intelligence, who have a high degree of social awareness and empathy, are better able to pick up on the discomfort of their peers and can help those who are silent to find a voice. They are also more effective at resolving conflicts, which could mean interceding on behalf of a team member who is being judged or punished.

Emotional intelligence is something Adrian Locher of Merantix values highly. 'We have several methods to test the EQ of a potential candidate,' he says. 'One is that we get the candidate interviewed by lots of different people from our team. Not only the team we are hiring into, but people from across the company. We make sure the candidate gets 360-degree assessment.'

There's more.

'We also have a very strict rule for the last stage of the hiring process which we call "on-site days". The candidate is required to spend two days with our teams and work on a specific topic and interact with lots of people during those two days. At the end we have an assessment which is astonishingly simple. Everyone who has interacted and worked with the candidate, which is called the hiring committee, has to vote yes or no. And there has to be 100 per cent consensus. There can't be one single objection.'

And if there is an objection?

'We have an in-depth discussion and we turn every stone. And I believe that in 95 per cent of the cases we reach consensus.'

Like Locher, Adnan Raza, CFO at PDF Solutions in California, USA, also looks for a combination of skill and emotional intelligence in new staff.

'When I hire people, I'm really looking for two things. First, I'm looking for the technical skills to be able to do the job – those can be taught if they don't have that. They should definitely have the foundational skills. What I am really looking for is the DNA for success. That is the number one thing for me. Do you have self-awareness to ask yourself, how can I get better? How can I continue to grow? "Tell me about the time when you made a mistake and how did you handle that?" We all make mistakes every day and you can't feel sorry for yourself for every mistake. You have to learn and move on.

'This is about the IQ bucket.'

But bucket number two is far more interesting, he says.

THE EMOTIONAL INTELLIGENCE BUCKET

'In the second piece of my interview, I always tell them, "I don't care about the topic. You pick the topic, but come and present to me something you're passionate about." It could be automobiles, it could be travel, it could be sport. It doesn't matter to me. What I'm trying to assess is the EQ of the person. How passionate are they about what about they are presenting? What are the reasons for their passion? Are they thinking about their passion holistically, rationally? Can they defend their passion?'

Raza will often disagree with the presenter violently to see how they react. 'I will challenge them and make a statement completely opposite of what they passionately believe. By the time we are done with the second interview, about an hour or more, I have a good sense.'

This two-stage interview enables Raza to make astute assessments. 'I found this two-level interview process, IQ and EQ, to be the best way to get to know people,' he says. 'Especially the EQ interview. How they engage, how they defend their position, and how they build a relationship with me and their engagement.'

Why go through all of this?

'EQ is what is important in the work environment. The technical skills are always changing anyway, you can learn them. But the EQ skills? You definitely need in life to be successful in anything you do.'

The new generation of leaders are very clear that they don't just interview and hire for technical, skill or competency fit. They also look for the culture fit – alignment of purpose, mission, values, and goals. They test for whether a candidate has emotional intelligence – are they connected with their own passion and purpose? They understand that you can have the smartest AI engineer or data scientist in the world, but if they don't connect with the company's vision, purpose, and values, they are not going to put their heart and soul into achieving that vision and aligning their actions with the values.

Putting the effort into building successful teams is one thing. But there's an even greater challenge for the New Leaders of Change. What impact they can make on the organization as a whole? ■

"When you are going through transformation, you have to recognize that the current systems of decision-making are influenced and framed by the current business context and the current business mindset. That is when your commitment to the new vision and your conviction is tested. Are you willing to move the organization towards the future state?

Christy Lake
Chief People Officer
Twilio

Chapter 8

TRANSFORMING THE 21ST CENTURY ORGANIZATION

How the New Leaders of Change make an organization-level impact

Most organizations aren't static. Even the largest continually change and evolve. But many times I have seen transformational leaders in traditional companies fail, in spite of possessing strong conviction, commitment, courage, and charisma.

I once worked with a very smart and passionate executive, Steve, from a major American technology company. He was a rising star who had been hired away from a competitor to help the company transform into a digital transformation service provider versus the traditional outsourcing services the firm offered.

Steve was an adamant proponent of digitalization. He had successfully helped another company, a competitor, to transform into a digital transformation service provider before taking on this new role and he knew he was critical to the long-term success of his new company.

When he started in his new role, he hit the ground running, and I was assigned as his onboarding coach.

I was impressed with his confidence, and his capability and ability to mobilize cross-functional teams without a direct reporting line. As his coach, I felt I was learning more from him than coaching him. He seemed to be doing all the right things. He recruited and hired some of the top digital transformation consultants into the company.

However, after some time, I realized that other senior leaders in the organization were uncomfortable with the pace of change and the exploration of new digital solutions with which they were not personally familiar.

Steve was charged with reaching out to the top 100 accounts to share how we could help them with their digital transformations. His drive, conviction, and passion captured the imagination of the account teams and some of the customers. But the account executives internally were feeling lost and out of control. It wasn't that they disagreed with what he was doing, but they were worried about the speed of change and what it might mean to the traditional outsourcing business where the company had excelled for decades.

It wasn't long before disagreements, fears for the future of the business, and finger-pointing flared up about the pace of change and the lack of rapid growth in the digital business. And 18 months after joining, Steve parted ways with the company.

What went wrong?

Steve had several traits that were widely considered important for someone leading digital transformation efforts for the company. He was courageous and confident in his ability and beliefs. He was decisive and action-oriented. He had the leadership charisma to inspire team members, partners, and customers with his vision. But these traits were not enough in the face of the organizational, business, and political complexity of traditional corporations.

One of Steve's biggest blind spots was that he perhaps should have realized that a rapid pivot from being an outsourcing company to a digital transformation service provider would meet resistance from leaders who had been in the company for decades. After all, they had successfully grown the company in the very outsourcing market Steve was trying to cannibalize. He thought he could convince them of his approach by using market and customer data, together with a combination of his logic and his charisma. But he did not appreciate or explore the executives' deeply held values, or their pride and emotional attachment to the business they had developed. Perhaps he wasn't even aware of them. Nor did he take account of the importance they placed on meeting their quarterly revenue objectives. Neither did he spot their low tolerance for risk.

After many discussions with Steve, I realized that he had expected the transformational leadership to come from the executives who brought him in. He assumed they would cover his back and he would just be able to leverage their leadership power to implement their joint vision.

So let's look at the systemic changes that the New Leaders of Change are introducing into their organizations – things including leading by values and leading with purpose – philosophies at the core of people-centered leadership.

Because the message Steve takes away from his experience is that organization-level change is hard, even when it's the right thing to do. And that it's the people-centered side of things that eventually let him down. That proved especially true in the face of the multi-generational leaders involved, who very likely built the business in the first place. We'll come back to Steve and what he could have done differently at the end of this chapter.

Not everything Steve did was problematic. He did have the curiosity to experiment, to think differently, and to act with courage, commitment, conviction, and charisma to inspire others. And that was good. These are, after all, key characteristics for leading transformation. But while these are natural attributes for entrepreneurial leaders, they are foreign bodies in traditional companies. And inside traditional organizations, the response to transformational ideas and transformational leadership is usually a full onslaught of antibodies to protect the *status quo.*

In other words, during times of change, when there is high uncertainty and the perceived prospect of winners and losers, there is a huge amount of political activity.

'LEADERSHIP IS NOT A GIFT'

It's for this reason that leadership is a real challenge, says Nirupa Chander, Managing Director, Singapore, for Hitachi ABB Power Grids. 'Leadership is not a gift,' she says.

When she was relocated to Singapore from Australia, she was pregnant with her second child. 'This role was a big challenge,' she says. 'It was not easy coming into a mostly traditional male Singaporean team and take on the top leadership role.'

Being attuned to how big a deal her appointment was, and showing huge self-awareness, she consciously put her ego aside, she says. 'I could not think that just because these people now report to me they will automatically follow my lead and work hard, focus, and follow my vision and direction with commitment. They really have to believe in you. I found that a big challenge.'

Her second challenge was dealing with power dynamics and political behaviors as the transformation took hold.

At the core the company was changing its organizational structure – from being country-focused to being product-focused. Of course, a global, product-focused organization, operating in a matrix structure, required different leadership capabilities, she says, such as leading through influence and empowerment.

'In the old model, every unit had a direct reporting line to the country manager. That meant that the country manager was like the God there. They had all the power. And suddenly we went into a vertical global organization, where the country management organization was responsible for certain outcomes, but only through a dotted line.'

She pauses, reflecting on how the former leaders in the country organization, mostly men, who had solid reporting lines, suddenly lost their power. In the Asian culture they were perceived as having lost face, she said.

'It was emotionally difficult for me because I was wondering about how it was being seen. They just felt insecure. And then they started doing things, you know, just to hoard power. The organizational antibodies kicked in just to protect their power and *status quo*. They found other ways to exert influence and power. And they were in that process losing credibility.'

It begs the question, how does behavior like this help an organization? Short answer: it doesn't.

'They were not working towards the company's actual strategy, which is to deliver more value to customers and drive growth. This global product set-up makes sense, but for it to be adopted, the people have to believe in it.' And that takes leadership work. It takes leaders who are self-aware and can show empathy and generosity towards others. Leaders who can treat people with dignity, fairness, and respect through the change process – as Chander did.

When I asked Chander what she learned through this difficult process, she paused for some time.

'My first challenging assignment as a young leader was where I had to test my own leadership skills,' she says. 'My learning in management early on was to focus on the human side of business and I believed in my capability to build a great team.'

At the time, she did this very intuitively, she says. It wasn't planned.

'Fast forward to now and it has always been important to me to articulate a collective vision and have the team move towards that direction – make sure we are all clear on what are we really working towards and why.'

Once these conditions are in place, says Chander, individuals inevitably feel empowered and a team feels cohesive.

'I feel we can achieve most audacious goals now and not be afraid to change, innovate, and grow.'

With that as her personal context, her learning is clear, she says.

'I think the people and the talent side is probably the most important thing because at the end of the day, an organization is a collection of human beings and minds and it's amazing.'

It's a philosophy that has consequences though, she says.

'If it's the people part that's the most important, then the other thing I learned was that when you have a non-team player, a non-performer, you have to address it right away.'

There's another pause.

'I made the mistake once of waiting for a time and giving someone a chance.'

But now?

'Don't wait for it because the dynamic is like a poison. Not only is that individual not performing, but they are also demotivating others. Taking action quickly on things that are not working builds your credibility and trust with the team.'

And it's this combination of lessons that crystallizes her current belief – that when you put the right team together, they can do the unthinkable.

'So I think to just continue focusing on the people and the talent aspect of change is really important.'

Even though we keep hearing about technology and AI, and that people will be replaced with robots?

'We're not going to be able to replace our fundamental emotional intelligence – the human side of things,' she says.

Chander demonstrates the power that a single strong individual has to change things. But what is becoming even clearer in the 21st century is how we need to move away from the idea that a single leader can change everything and embed a set of values and indeed a purpose across entire organizations.

TOWARD THE PURPOSE-DRIVEN ORGANIZATION

Katie Koch, Co-Head of Fundamental Equity at Goldman Sachs Asset Management, says purpose-driven leadership has helped her in many difficult turnaround situations.

'I think you have to set the right tone, a shared purpose, the right set of shared values,' she says. 'You have to keep coming back to that.'

Why?

'The markets will go up, and they will go down. Some of your investment decisions for clients will work out spectacularly well and others may not go your way. So you need a sense of shared purpose and values to come back to when you are trying to navigate out of some challenging situations.'

The company decided to organize itself around a set of values, she says. 'The values were humility, collaboration, and diversity of thought. That's what carried us through the change.'

It's important to take notice of what Koch says. She's not talking about achieving change at an entrepreneurial start-up. Goldman Sachs Asset Management is one of the world's leading asset managers with a big company DNA. Koch was hired to help lead a turnaround of the organization's equity business and she was able to catalyze change with a people-centered approach.

If you have a big company's DNA, you need to catalyze strategic changes – small mutations that make it possible for a start-up model and mindset to thrive inside a much different species.

'In the asset management business, the goal is to generate performance above and beyond market benchmarks in your investment strategies and, on the back of creating value, to raise assets,' she explains. 'This business had only 15 per cent of strategies outperforming their respective benchmarks and it was losing assets. So that is the evidence that the business was broken and that's where we were.'

That was three years ago – where is Fundamental Equity now?

'To give you a headline of where we got to in three years: we now have 90 per cent of strategies outperforming benchmarks and the business is having our best year. In addition, we were able to accomplish this in a shrinking industry, which has its own challenges.'

There's something worth adding here. Even though it took courage to embark on such a transformation, the business had hit an acute change-or-die moment. They knew they had to take drastic action, there was no choice but to change.

'It is a little bit daunting at the beginning,' she says. 'But the upside of it is also liberating, because you can't do a lot to make it worse. You can actually expand your set of options dramatically. You can take more risks and have a completely different frame of mind.'

That also takes courage, though.

'Yes, that also takes courage because people in the business are still afraid of change – humans are always afraid of change.' But they were prepared to make the change because they wanted to get out of the current situation, she says.

Koch's approach to the successful turnaround of the Fundamental Equity business was multi-pronged. However, she believes the key was an intentional focus on creating the environment and culture for change.

'It was a really challenging situation, but we said, "okay, we're going to do some stuff differently and new,"' she says. So they started with culture – their vision and values.

Doing something different and new doesn't simply mean introducing new products or markets. After 25 years working with organizations and senior leaders, I've come to believe that organizations don't transform, people do. I have witnessed over the years, that it isn't a lack of information on technology, customer or competitive trends that holds people back. It isn't access to technology or capital. (There is plenty of this in the right circumstances.) It is the fear of undertaking the leadership necessary to embark on the transformation journey. And that fear is both personal – we ask ourselves 'am I up to this?' – and professional. (We ask ourselves how will this affect my role or my future prospects?) And ultimately these twin fears rob us of the will to commit to a bold vision and to follow through with courage.

Which is why Twilio's Christy Lake is clear about this: at some point you will be tested, she says.

'When you are going through transformation, you have to recognize that the current systems of decision-making are influenced and framed by the current business context and the current business mindset,' she says. 'That is when your commitment to the new vision and your conviction is tested.'

And I conclude that the tests Lake poses raise further questions. For example, how willing are you to stand firm, to have courage in the face of your uncertain future, and to make the difficult choices you're going to have to? How much do you personally believe in the future vision of the firm? So that you can make it come alive for everyone involved? And how much are you committed to take the bold action and decisions necessary to move the organization into the future?

What I'm saying is this is in large measure about your conviction and your intentions. Because if you're going to use values as a key driver of change in the 21st century, it is important to do this intentionally.

TOWARD THE VALUES-DRIVEN ORGANIZATION

One company that does intentional values-based leadership well is Salesforce, a cloud-based CRM software platform.

'At Salesforce, our leadership team were as intentional about the culture they wanted to create as they were about the products they wanted to build,' says Stephen Baines, Lead Solutions Consultant for Salesforce in the UK.

And being intentional about creating and using a positive organizational culture brings many benefits. First, because the firm undertakes organizational change frequently, in part because of the rapid growth of the company. 'Almost every year we make structural changes,' says Baines. 'It is really executed well,' he says, 'because Salesforce has a culture of trust, customer success, diversity, equality, and innovation.'

Changes are communicated in advance, for example, and decisions include the groups that are affected by change. There's a good deal of engagement, he says, and people are involved throughout.

'It's not leaving things in the dark,' he says, 'it's about being open, transparent and giving people a clear vision of the shared future and how we will get there.'

One of the reasons this seems to work for Salesforce is the use of a standardized process for cascading its core values across the company.[33]

'What I love about Salesforce is our unwavering commitment to our core values, which have been the foundation of our company since day one. We call it V2MOM and it's a process for alignment for every major company decision at Salesforce.'[34]

V2MOM was first developed and introduced by founder Marc Benioff almost at the company's founding in 1999 and it's still in use today. So it's worth investigating if you haven't come across it already.

There is another set of values which the New Leaders of Change are increasingly embodying – the values of the start-up organization.

Organizations, like living organisms, have a life cycle, composed of four broad phases:

- The **Start-up** phase
- The **Growth** phase
- The **Sustain** or **Plateau** phase
- The **Reinvention** or **Rebirth** phase

Now, each phase has unique needs when it comes to change, transformation, and leadership. But if you're looking for organizations defined by a philosophy of how they operate, consider start-ups. These are organizations we can learn huge lessons from when it comes to leading change. Of course, what I'm really suggesting is that we look initially at the leaders of those start-ups, because it's they who embody the start-up mentality and the start-up culture.

We've already met Jonas Muff, CEO and founder of Vara, a Berlin-based med-tech company that builds AI solutions for medical imaging. When we were looking at multi-generational leadership in Chapter

Table 5: Salesforce's model for cascading vision and values

1. Vision — what do you want to achieve?
2. Values — what's important to you?
3. Methods — how do you get it?
4. Obstacles — what is preventing you from being successful?
5. Measures — how do you know you have it?

Salesforce's vision and values methodology, V2MOM, was first developed in 1999 and is still in use today – it's worth investigating for that reason alone

4. And I want to reintroduce him here because he has already been the CEO of two start-ups. In his very short leadership journey to date, he's had his share of change, ambiguity, ups-and-downs, and character-building challenges. But one of the fascinating things he shares is that he finds it hard to understand the concept of managing change.

'I have a natural reaction to the phrase "change management". I don't get what it actually means.'

Curious, I ask him why.

'Everything is change in a start-up. Everything we do is about changing something. It's a natural process of iterating. In a start-up everything iterates.'

Then he says something that grips me.

'It's about changing ourselves.'

Putting that idea to one side for a moment, I put this to him. That if everything is always changing, how does everything align and how does he get the results he hopes for?

'The key is to find the people that are willing to change constantly,' he says, highlighting again the significance of having the right people in the right roles.

'If an employee in the business development area gets a negative reaction from the market and loses motivation, then they are the wrong person. But in a start-up what you need is a person that says "okay, I hit the wall. Let me try the next wall, or the door on the left or the right and eventually I'll get there." Hiring the right person is crucial.'

But once you have the right people in place then communication becomes central in a start-up, he says. It's important in every firm, but it's mission critical in a start-up.

'When the processes change, when the vision and goals change, you need to communicate. It sounds super trivial, but it is not, because you need to craft and deliver the right message to the right people.' So part of encouraging a start-up culture is to encourage a culture of communication, where your team knows they will be informed when something changes.

'For example, when our fundraising didn't go as planned, we sat down with everybody and told them "it's not going well". These are the reasons, we said, and these are the plans we have to address "the concerns" and we will talk to them again in two weeks. That kind of open communication creates trust and employees understand and expect that in these situations the leaders and management will inform and be transparent.'

So I ask him what communication looks like in a start-up culture.

'We communicate in a very agile way. We don't do all-hands type of meeting. We communicate more through deep-dive reviews or spotlights on certain topics. We sit down with the relevant people and talk to them. We talk in smaller groups.'

They also communicate via the Slack platform and with other written forms of communication. 'Because we expect everyone to be open to change which brings me back to hiring the right people again.'

So can he sum up the start-up culture so that others can replicate it in whichever organization they are?

'It's about hiring, communication, and culture,' he says.

TOWARD NETWORKED STRUCTURES

Another element of the start-up culture that's being adopted more broadly by the New Leaders of Change is the flat structure. This is significant because flatter organizations communicate laterally, without unnecessary hierarchy, and this enables them to adapt to change in a more fluid and flexible way. This is in stark contrast to the traditional organizational structure, with its heavily bureaucratic culture, where command-and-control is the order of the day. Don't get me wrong – hierarchical structures and reporting were useful when efficiency, speed, and accuracy were the backbone of most organizations. But that isn't the case any longer.

The unfortunate fact is that people who grew up leading traditional organizations are not comfortable with the start-up mentality of flatter organizations. They seem concerned that flatter structures will create confusion – by not having clearly defined management structures, or by allowing people to fail without fear of reprisal. And by allowing the easy questioning of authority, many from the hierarchical world feel their power and status are threatened.

When Anne-Sophie d'Andlau, Co-founder of CIAM asset management, decided to start her own investment firm with offices in Paris and London she began to pitch to investors for seed money, as you would expect. But their proposed organizational, leadership structure, and governance models were rejected by numerous traditional investors.

'When my partner Catherine Berjal and I decided to create this business 10 years ago, we put together a very different organizational structure,' she says. 'It was not vertical, it was horizontal.'

In a horizontal structure, she says, everyone knows what decisions they are accountable for and what decisions are being made.

'When we went to investors for seed money, one investor said, "I am not going to give you any seed money because your governance structure can't work. You want to create a fund with two people at the top, you are going to fight, you are going to battle, at the end of the day it can't work."

'So they passed over us because of this specific difference in our leadership structure. We did prove them wrong because today we are a very successful fund and we are still leading the business together.'

WHAT'S MORE RADICAL THAN A FLAT STRUCTURE?

Hard though it may be to believe, there is an organizational structure even more radical than the flat structure. Holacracy, developed by Brian Robertson and Tom Thomison, which is a form of organization that adopts a constitution, has its own by-laws and offers a fairly egalitarian organizational culture.[35]

Thomas Klein, People and Organization Leader of Jodel, a Berlin start-up focused on building local communities, remembers his first leadership role as an HR leader helping the organization to adopt Holacracy.

'My first leadership role was in an innovation agency in Berlin and they were in the midst of changing their organizational model to Holacracy, a radical "self-governing" operating system, where there were no job titles and no managers. Instead of a top-down hierarchy, there's a flatter "holarchy" that distributes power more evenly to self-directed teams.'

I ask him how does Holacracy work?

'It starts with the CEO taking a step back and giving all the responsibility and accountability to the self-directed teams and roles.'

That sounds different. 'It is very different, but it's a structured approach,' he says. 'It requires teams and people to take accountability for their work and leadership is distributed into each role.'

So everybody is expected to lead and to be almost an entrepreneur in their own roles?

'Yes, and Holacracy empowers them to do so. In fact, the teams are structured into circles, so it was definitely a very different model than what I learned in business psychology.'

Klein learned a great deal about Holacracy as he was responsible for building up the HR department and aligning its processes with the Holacracy operating model. But it wasn't easy.

'I was struggling with how to adopt HR processes to Holacracy and how to do HR in an agile way. That was also the first time where the CEO told me: "You make the decisions – you decide how we are going to set up the HR structure and processes." And this was not even one year after my graduation. It was amazing, giving the whole responsibility and decision-making power to the employees versus top-down.'

It's clear that Klein's leadership experience certainly wasn't gathered in a traditional corporate environment. He's now worked in various start-ups and is running his own company so his leadership style appears deeply entrepreneurial. Given that background, I ask him to define what a start-up culture looks like.

'The start-up model is continuously questioning and challenging your assumptions while keeping a close eye on the market and the pulse of the customer,' he says.

'To operate like a start-up, you need an organizational model that is like a fluid system, like an organism that continuously interacts with the external environment, and understand what kind of influences are coming into the system.' It really is like something living, he says.

'And then, the organism is able to adjust, change, and reiterate itself depending on what influences are coming in from the outside world.' It's a naturally agile system.

He understands how overwhelming this appears to a traditional leader. 'It might sound a bit frustrating or overwhelming or stressful, but that's the world today. You have to compete with other companies in the market. You want to stay on top. You have to always be reachable. You have to challenge and question yourself every day and find the best way to solve the problems. Every day.'

Despite the trend towards the flatter structure preferred by start-ups and by the New Leaders of Change, it would be wrong to say one structure or another is the single best structure to adopt. Because there are no perfect organizational models. Even a system based on a hierarchy can have its benefits. For example, there are some purely digital-first companies using some form of hierarchical structure as they scale, with a combination of functional and product-based organizational models. However, you do hear them use the term 'flat hierarchy', rather than hierarchy. While start-ups want the benefits associated with this form of organization, they also want to minimize the number of layers that might emerge and a growing middle management.

So new generation leaders understand the risks associated with rigid and rule-based hierarchical organizations. And they try to mitigate those risks by the intentional development of a culture that values cross-functional teamwork and lateral communications, as well as preserving the decision rights of everyone, regardless of title and seniority. It's a learning journey and it's probably fair to say that the new generation leaders are more open to exploring new and hybrid organizational forms, keeping what works and discarding what doesn't.

Nevertheless, a trend is emerging. The new generation of leaders broadly seem to prefer start-up environments to that of the monolithic traditional corporation. According to media reports over the last few years one in three Millennials recommends working for start-ups; 60 per cent consider themselves entrepreneurs with ideas, concepts, and plans; while 71 per cent would prefer to quit their jobs and work for themselves.[36]

And so companies that don't respond to the call for change will soon fall behind and alienate their most valuable asset, this new generation of leaders, and employees. For example, Katy Hutchinson is a Senior Equity Research Analyst at Impax Asset Management.

Hutchinson started her career in a traditional investment firm, but soon found herself alienated and not having the opportunity to contribute to her fullest potential.

'I was the only female analyst in my firm across 20 analysts. In finance, accounting firms can be quite old-school, super political and male dominated. And I was the only one under the age of 30, which was quite daunting. There was a big age and generational difference.'

How was that experience, I ask.

'It was quite a challenge,' she says. 'One of the first things I learned was the saying "clients love gray hair," which is an awful thing.' There was a strong belief that older people have more experience and give better advice. And that affected Hutchinson deeply.

'It is quite frustrating as a young analyst, because you see it internally in the firm's culture, you see it with your institutional clients, you see it with your corporate clients. And, especially as a young woman, it's hard to kind of break that mold and be empowered and say "I deserve to be here," "I have something to say."'

She stuck with the firm as long as she could, hoping things might improve, but she soon felt the need to make a change.

'I worked in that firm for a few years and really understood what it means to have a "legacy mindset". I began to reflect and to question my future. "Am I going to stay here a decade, or two decades, and eventually take on the most important stocks? Am I going to wait it out and wait for my turn to come? Is this what I studied to do?" And I said no! I wanted to get closer to the action. I wanted to make my own decisions in terms of investing.'

The other lack Hutchinson felt was that her current role didn't involve sustainable investing.

'And it was about that time that I got an email from a headhunter and took a job with an investment firm called Impax Asset Management. It is a sustainable asset manager and that area was really close to my heart. It was divine timing.'

EXODUS OF THE ENTREPRENEURS

As well as rising stars like Hutchinson, who leave to go to other employers, there will be others who may well leave old-school employers to launch their own businesses – if, that is, the dyed-in-the-wool traditional organizations don't change fast enough. And the scale of the exodus could be devastating.

'Studies have shown that some 70 per cent of Millennials either already identify themselves as entrepreneurs, or believe that they will someday become one, rejecting more traditional jobs to lead their own thing,' says Tristan Jackson, Chief Strategy Officer and Co-founder of Veckta, an international energy solutions company.

'Of course, that is unrealistic – it's mathematically impossible for seven out of 10 people to lead their own business,' he says. 'But, as business leaders, we need to look at why so many people want to be entrepreneurs. The potential to make a lot of money is part of it, but only part. Even more than money, we Millennials want autonomy, we want to bring our authentic selves to work, we want greater purpose and meaning in the work we are doing.'

Most Millennials want to achieve more than just shareholder profit, then?

'Right. We want to work for companies that contribute to restoring the environment and the communities we operate in. We don't feel like we have much real opportunity for that in the traditional corporate world. It's not that those organizations don't exist, but they're very scarce. It can be disheartening.'

And that isn't something firms want to have happen. Because if Millennials and Generation Z employees aren't engaged and inspired at work, they're likely to be checked out. And that's a problem that can have a direct impact on a company's profitability, productivity, innovation, and capacity to adapt to external changes. According to data from the Gallup organization, the high level of job turnover among Millennials is estimated to cost the US economy well in advance of $30bn annually.[37]

So what can you, the next generation of leaders, do about this? Well, if you can help traditional companies change, you'll be able to achieve more of the things you care about.

'We need to come into these big existing organizations and be able to bring a new flavor, plant a new seed,' says Jackson. New leaders need to help organizations transform themselves for the future. 'Firms need to be a lot leaner, more flexible and more ecosystem-style, more platform-style, creating value for communities. They need to be less narrowly focused on quarterly results and shareholders.'

This is starting to happen, he says, but it needs to pick up pace.

CAUTION: START-UPS AREN'T ALWAYS GREAT

'There are a few little disruptive things happening out there, but a lot less than people might think. All the disruptive tech companies? As they grew, they didn't turn out that much different than the firms they replaced, in the way it feels to work inside of them. Corporate organizations that feel overly hierarchal and oppressive to their employees are due for disruption.'

So it isn't always the case that start-ups are great places to work. Sometimes it's just an image, a myth we have, of start-ups as a place of empowerment, creativity, rapid innovation, and the opportunity to work on a purpose that will make a real, positive change in the world. We've seen multiple headline stories in recent years of toxic start-up cultures, for example at Uber in the early days. But sometimes it's difficult to assess this from the outside.[38]

As a seasoned leader in companies such as Wipro, Infosys, Oracle, and DXC, Arpit Kaushik, CEO of Hypha, a UK-based innovation and consulting platform, has seen his fair share of bureaucracy, dysfunctional teams, and what he calls 'asshole' leaders.[39]

But Kaushik was taken completely by surprise when he did a short leadership stint in a start-up before joining Hypha as CEO.

'This was the most rigorous selection process I've ever had in my life, presenting to the board, 12 hours of interviews, meeting every member of the team.' He also attended their annual employee event and had a great time. 'And I was like, "wow, this culture looks great". So I joined them as their Chief Operating Officer responsible for building the products.'

So, how did it turn out?

'I came in with high expectations but false beliefs,' he says. Such as? 'Such as start-ups are about doing things that are smart, innovative, and cutting edge. Kind of similar to Silicon Valley standards. Very quickly I learned that I was in the wrong start-up.' In fact, Kaushik was shocked to see the team in action and that the way they worked seemed so backwards.

'Decisions were slow and painful. There was zero alignment. We were a 13-member executive team and everyone had a say in everything. No matter what your role or function were, you had decision-making power in everything that happened. Just to give you an example, they had made the decision to move from Dropbox to Sharepoint three years ago and it still hadn't got off the ground.' He shakes his head at the waste of it all.

'Imagine every day you had to convince 13 people and any one of them could have the veto. If one of them doesn't want to do it, it's not happening. So making any change was damn hard in that company.'

Not surprisingly, the company found itself in financial trouble in a very short time. 'They failed to get the next round of funding,' he says. 'I had to pretty much lay off my whole team. I was very disturbed and shared my people-centric leadership philosophy of trust, empathy, and vulnerability and its importance in such situations.'

What happened?

'The team were like "what a weirdo." That was the reaction.'

As always, passing through crucibles such as this, there is learning.

'One of my key learnings was that there are "assholes" in large companies and there are "assholes" in start-ups. So I stopped viewing large companies as "evils" and start-ups as the "saviors".'

Once again, it seems, a new generation leader realizes that creating a positive, uplifting culture is perhaps the single most important element for a leader.

'Regardless of how well you wish for your team, regardless of the results you want to achieve, regardless of what you want to create in this world… if the culture and environment is not there, you have no hope in the leadership.'

So he decided to create his own company. And that's when Hypha was born, to embody Kaushik's empathetic philosophy.

'This has always been my vision, since I started work in 2006. To create a different kind of company which is purposeful, compassionate, very people-centric and high-performing. You don't have to be an asshole to succeed in this world. You can be human-centric, you can be purpose-driven and you can achieve the best performance.'

The verdict is in: the New Leaders of Change featured in this book, and many others I haven't been able to include, are looking to work for people-centered organizations, regardless of whether it is a start-up or a traditional organization.

However, what New Leaders of Change also seem to be learning is that to systemically shift an organization's purpose and practices with impact requires a holistic approach to designing change – connecting people, process, workflow, and technology. There are no proven methods and roadmaps for shifting factory-model organizations to agile people-centered organizations that are fit for the 21st century.

This is not a trivial challenge. The problem facing slow-moving firms is huge. I shared a McKinsey report on this earlier, but according to market research firm IDC, 75 per cent of major enterprises are going to fail to meet their digital transformation targets.[40] My own research suggests that many of them are over-emphasizing the technology elements in transformation, paying insufficient attention to the leadership and people requirements that drive cultural and process change. Because making organizational change and transformation is a highly people-centric task. It's about engaging, inspiring, and motivating all those touched by change. The great news is that the New Leaders of Change intuitively and intellectually understand this – that successful change is about people and ensuring people understand the future vision, they are connected to the purpose of the change, and they are engaged in the change process.

And I've highlighted through this research some basic principles for initiating change toward becoming people-centric, agile, and resilient. For example, organizations can adopt, create, and thrive in new ways of working and innovating and thus making small but significant steps towards systemic transformations of the enterprise. Whether you're in an early-stage start-up just thinking about building your culture, or in a traditional organization and seeking to refresh and be future ready, these principles can help you orient, be more thoughtful in your approach to transformation, and keep people at the center of your plans.

NOW IS THE TIME

Without having people at the core of your plans for change, change will not be successful. This is because organizations are complex. They have social, technical, economic, and cultural aspects as well as a political dimension all vying with each other to drive the organization forward. But the transformation journey in any company disrupts many of these dimensions and success depends on many factors.

However, true transformation cannot occur if people are not fully invested in it. Regardless of the transformation strategy and methods utilized, it's becoming more important to engage the people who are involved and impacted – customers, employees, shareholders, and stakeholders – when making decisions about change, transformation, and implementation strategy. Organizations need to engage the hearts, minds, and passion of all individuals and teams involved in change.

The environment created by exponential changes – volatile, uncertain, complex, and ambiguous – is the challenge and opportunity of our times. And the time for organizations to organize for speed, innovation, change, and resilience is now. This will be a long process and leaders must leap into the arena and recognize that many of their familiar organization constructs will need to be reimagined.

Companies will want to seize the moment to reimagine and reinvent the future, building new muscle and capabilities to come back strong. Even well-run companies may find that they need to reinvent themselves more than once.

Fortune will favor the bold – and the speedy.

Let's conclude this overview of the strategies and approaches of the New Leaders of Change by looking back at Steve, who we started this chapter with. Knowing what we know now about organization-level change, what could he have done that would have helped him?

Steve could have approached his role as the transformation leader from a people-centered perspective. Involve key stakeholders and keep people at the center of the change process. He could have realized the right conditions for such a business transformation – transitioning from legacy outsourcing services to offering digital transformation services – were not there. The leadership team was paralyzed by bureaucracy, misaligned goals, competing strategies, and fear of losing power. How might Steve unite this team to work together towards a new future and harness their collective energy to embark on the transformation process?

At the core of people-centered change is the principle that people support what they co-create. Steve could have engaged the leadership team with a new sense of vision and purpose toward the future state of the business – as a digital transformation services provider. He could have engaged the leadership team on designing a strategy and a plan for transitioning the legacy outsourcing business to digital transformation services.

Unfortunately, however, he was unaware of these hidden forces ranged against him and ultimately succumbed to what I like to describe as the corporate antibodies, which crowded him out of his role.

And while these organizational antibodies are highly effective at killing new ideas inside traditional companies, the New Leaders of Change are nevertheless overcoming them by dragging the top teams' attention away from the quarterly profits report and demanding that companies be built around purpose and values, as Chander and Koch demonstrate. And slowly, but with gathering speed as my research and the stories here demonstrate, the new generation of leaders are transforming the way organizations operate. Engaging and changing them, through steady innovations, to become a force for good. Something besides making a profit. Something good for the planet and something good for humanity. Now we have a new generation of leaders, customers, and employees who are increasingly expecting this and willing to make it a priority.

Because these younger leaders believe changing big business is not enough. They also want to change the world. And they are, as we'll see in the next chapter. ■

“I was always inspired to start my own business in the renewable energy industries versus taking on another corporate job somewhere and doing something meaningless. I wanted to live up to my motto of trying to save the planet.

Martin Baart
CEO
Ecoligo

Chapter 9

CHANGING THE WORLD

A purpose beyond business

When I was living in California's Silicon Valley, it was natural to be aware of and to practice sustainable living, as well as respect for the environment and social justice. My friends and I shopped at natural, organic grocery shops and farmers' markets. We avoided fast food, excessive sugar, most meat, and the consumer mindset. Admittedly, my children, growing up in the 1990s and 2000s, felt somewhat deprived for not taking part in the American tradition of fast, processed food, especially when McDonald's and others began giving away plastic toys with children's Happy Meals.

Fast forward 30 years, I was on a project with two Millennial colleagues, both in their early 30s. One day during lunch break they said that they were going to walk over to the McDonald's in the next block and asked if I wanted to join them. Horrified, I started to lecture them about how McDonald's is unhealthy, processed foods are unsustainable, their use of plastic is not good for the environment, and so on.

My colleagues, with an amused look on their faces, began to educate me about the actions McDonald's was taking on the sustainability front. It has aggressive sustainability goals, actions, and metrics and is taking it all very seriously. For example, it is continually increasing recycling, reducing and eliminating use of plastic, and aims to get 100 per cent of its food sources from sustainable production.

I am not advocating that we all start eating at McDonald's – I just want to point out how the focus on sustainability and Corporate Social Responsibility has permeated even the fast-food industry.

Sustainability, and social and environmental responsibility, are no longer a fad or a trend. Corporate Social Responsibility (CSR) and Environment, Society, and Governance (ESG) initiatives are becoming necessary to compete and succeed in today's business world.

Even though the concepts of Corporate Social Responsibility and sustainability have been evolving since the 1960s, it has always been more of a fringe movement. The dominant thinking about the role of business, as expressed by Milton Friedman, the Nobel Prize-winning economist, was simple and easy to understand: 'There is one and only one social responsibility of business – to use its resources and engage in activities designed to increase its profits.'[41] Companies, in the prevailing view, must make money for their shareholders.

Over the following decades the primacy of shareholders was the sole focus and purpose of business. In 1997, this philosophy was reinforced by Business Roundtable, an association of over 200 American CEOs, in their formal statement of corporate purpose: 'The paramount duty of management and of boards of directors is to the corporation's stockholders.'

WHAT IS THE PURPOSE OF A CORPORATION?

In 2019, however, the Business Roundtable made a dramatic shift in redefining the purpose of a corporation.[42] They extended the breadth of the corporation's duty to a broader set of stakeholders, including employees, customers, suppliers, and the broader community.

Since then, Larry Fink, CEO of Blackrock, the largest asset manager in the world with more than $7 trillion under management, made a strong case in his 2020 letter to CEOs that climate change would fundamentally reshape the world of finance.[43]

In the same year, the World Economic Forum published its Davos Manifesto, *The Universal Purpose of a Company in the Fourth Industrial Revolution*, stating, 'The purpose of a company is to engage all its stakeholders in shared and sustained value creation. In creating such value, a company serves not only its shareholders, but all its stakeholders – employees, customers, suppliers, local communities and society at large.'[44]

And the CEOs of roughly 200 European companies announced

that they would be calling on the three European Union leaders at the time, Ursula von der Leyen, Charles Michel and David Maria Sassoli – presidents of the European Commission, the Council of the European Union and the European Parliament, respectively – to implement an overarching strategy for a Sustainable Europe by 2030.

This is a powerful narrative, shifting the purpose of the corporation and definition of value creation to include a wide range of stakeholders and pressing environmental and societal issues.

The question is: why have attitudes begun to change only now?

The key reason is that the new generation, the Millennials and Generation Z, no longer want to work for, invest in or buy from companies that focus only on profits and shareholder value.

They actively make it clear that the current economic system represents a betrayal of environment and of society. And, at last, CEOs and investors are recognizing that their businesses' long-term success is closely linked to environmental sustainability, and to human beings – their customers, employees, suppliers, and local communities.

Now Millennials and Generation Z are holding these companies to their words, as leaders, employees, consumers, investors, and community members. They are demanding systemic changes and longer-term thinking, and they fight for policies – both from governments and businesses – that protect people and the planet. Otherwise, they say, what you promise is just empty rhetoric.

One of those new leaders is Linda Dörig of Gebana in Burkina Faso. What the Business Roundtable and the World Economic Forum are now calling for is old news to her.

'I think we should be less focused on just making money and focus more on meeting the needs of the stakeholders – employees, suppliers, and local community,' she says.

Like many other new-generation leaders she believes that companies can do more than just make money. They can aspire to solve the big issues of environment and society and improve the state of the world. They can stand for something bigger with their products and services.

'At Gebana, we are a profit-making company,' says Dörig. 'We are not an NGO. And as a company you have to make money to be a viable business: to invest, to manage risks, fix quality problems, and pay your employees and suppliers fair wages. However, money should not be the main focus or the starting point.'

Gebana has its origins in the Swiss women's movement in the 1970s. Today, it is a growing company working closely with organic family farmers in Europe, Africa, and South America. Through Gebana, these families sell products such as organic fruits – fresh and dried, nuts, and cereals like soy and cocoa directly to customers in Europe.

Dörig took over as CEO of Gebana Burkina Faso in 2016 when the company was close to bankruptcy due to mismanagement, poor harvests, and escalation of prices. Since then, together with investors, customers, and more than 2,800 individual end customers, she has successfully rehabilitated the subsidiary.

But for her it has never been about the financial rewards of turning the business round.

'I don't think you should approach a job saying, I want to have a package of benefits worth $500,000 and then I will do this and that,' she says. 'I think you should approach a job asking some key questions like: What is the higher purpose of what the company is trying to achieve? What are the resources to achieve that purpose? What benefits does this company bring to employees and communities? Does it benefit people or not?'

And if it doesn't, what then?

'If it does not bring benefits to people and society, you have to change something because, in the long-run, the business is not viable.'

As a company, Gebana considers itself to be a network of customers, farmers, and partners who share the vision of fair trade. It forms value chains spanning from family farmers to customers in the most direct way possible, aiming to maximize the social and environmental value, creating jobs in countries of origin, and investing with a long-term perspective, often in difficult regions.

For example, Gebana in Switzerland says it has started to pay 10 per cent of the sales price in its online shop to family farmers. In 2020, it says, it paid over €530,000 (over $600,000), to farming families, in addition to the purchase price and organic and fair trade premiums. It's a real helping hand.

Organizations like Gebana with a social purpose are committed to aligning and integrating all their stakeholders' interests into the fabric of their corporate strategy, culture, and operations. Their leaders are driven by the company's social purpose and they are passionate about serving their employees, partners, shareholders, community, and the environment. They have a transparent, authentic, trusting, and human-centric culture where people aspire to create value for all their stakeholders.

And increasingly in charge of these businesses are the New Leaders of Change. They lead their lives and businesses with purpose, passion, and creativity.

'WE HAVE THE RESPONSIBILITY'

'I'm driven by my goal to save the planet as I believe we have not only the opportunity but also the responsibility to take more action,' says Martin Baart of Ecoligo. 'With this goal in mind, I am pioneering the global energy transition in emerging markets with our team.'

Baart has more than 14 years of experience in the renewable energy industry, with more than 10 years in emerging markets. He started his career in Australia working for Powercorp, focusing on grid integration, solar energy, and the technical integration of solar and wind solutions into microgrids for remote communities.

When Powercorp was acquired by ABB, he realized that large corporates were not actually where he wanted to spend his time. He joined a Berlin start-up called One Shore Energy. 'I particularly got interested in their idea of bringing finance to off-grid projects and basically building up an independent power producer,' he says.

He was with them for two years as Chief Technology Officer before founding Ecoligo to focus more strongly on the financing element. Ecoligo provides a fully financed solar-as-a-service solution for businesses in emerging markets, with a complete digital platform for financing and delivering solar projects.

'When we started Ecoligo, my co-founder and I had actually been traveling rather frequently to Africa. We really thought we would see a lot of solar projects being implemented in Kenya and in other countries in the region because conditions were just perfect.'

But they didn't. There were barely any solar projects, even though commercial and industrial clients in those countries were being charged high energy tariffs by the government.

'It turns out that businesses didn't want to invest their own capital in implementing solar energy. They saw the benefits of solar, yes, but whenever they had extra cash available, they invested in their core business. And on top of that, in those markets, there were basically no bank loans available.'

Baart realized that this was a huge obstacle – and that he could do something about it. 'If they would get a solution where they would have finance included, that would really help them make the decision. They wouldn't have to invest capital themselves, but they could benefit obviously from the savings on the energy cost.'

So he and his co-founder set up Ecoligo, which removes the initial cost and investment burden from customers by financing the solar projects through a crowd-investing platform, offering fixed returns to private investors. Investments start from E100 ($116) and save tons of carbon dioxide emissions. This allows small businesses run by local people to participate in a meaningful way in the global energy transition. And of course, supplying businesses with affordable electricity, the company says, enables them to grow. All of this boosts the local economy.

MEANINGLESS OR MEANINGFUL?

'I was always inspired to start my own business in the renewable energy industries versus taking on another corporate job somewhere and doing something meaningless,' says Baart. 'I wanted to live up to my motto of trying to save the planet.'

And in his own way he is.

'At Ecoligo, we help companies in the emerging markets save CO2. We want to focus on businesses because we believe businesses are the driver behind change, the driver behind employment and economic growth. And we want to focus on emerging markets because we think they're underrepresented and they need to grow sustainably.'

And they have a bold vision.

'Our vision is actually to empower all businesses in emerging markets to become CO2 neutral when it comes to energy. We're not finished when we have reached 1,000. We are not finished when we reached 10,000. We're finished when we have reached every single company in all emerging markets to be CO2 neutral. Once they all have an energy supply that is completely CO2 free, then we can stop.'

He pauses at the significance of what he's just said.

'That's probably going to take us a long time.'

In the same way Martin Baart is enabling other companies to change through financing, Andrea Ruotolo is helping other companies change through sharing her expertise.

Her mission, she says, is to help build more resilient energy systems in the face of new climate conditions and cyber-attacks. 'When we talk about climate conditions, we are mostly focused on reducing emissions, which is certainly very important. Reducing emissions is mitigating the impact of climate change. However, we hear much less about the fact that climate disruption is already here and will keep getting more extreme, no matter how quickly we reduce carbon emissions, and we need to talk about adaptation to the new climate conditions at the same time, while we work on mitigation.'

That sounds rather alarming.

'Yes, I think one of the reasons the topic of adaptation gets less attention than mitigation is that it can be overwhelming to think about. So part of what I work on is finding ways to talk about it that hopefully are less alarming, so we can face the issues and deal with them. Because as much as we do need renewable energy and need to reduce carbon emissions, we also need to adapt, and part of adaptation is that we need more resilient energy distribution systems.'

Distributed energy systems (DES) are relatively smaller systems, which include distributed solar power, batteries, generators, and micro-grids, located close to where they are needed. 'DES are very critical for urban centers,' she says.

'With centralized power grids, extreme weather events can cause widespread power outages, 90 per cent of which are caused by problems at the distribution level of the grid. In contrast, distributed energy systems can put energy supplies right where they are needed and can keep power on for critical facilities during the outages of the larger grid that do occur, because DES can also be used to help restore power to the larger grid after major events like storms and fires.'

Weather is a serious problem, she says. In Puerto Rico in 2017, the entire island lost power when it was hit by Hurricane Maria. 'Many people went for months without any electricity at all. The human and economic impact of not having electricity in a hot climate is devastating. With no refrigeration or air conditioning, and water pumps not working for months, the total cost to the economy and in human life may still not have been accounted for – by any account, it was certainly a terrible event.'

Despite the seriousness of the challenge, the importance of finding solutions as quickly as possible gives Ruotolo the energy that she brings to the conversation. The need to accelerate the energy transition to a lower-carbon and more resilient grid has given her a real sense of purpose. And for Ruotolo, business purpose inspires her to bring her undivided attention to solving difficult problems.

'Every now and then I have to come back to my center and remind myself of my mission and what brought me to this work in the first place. It is to ensure people and societies can be ready and resilient in the face of new threats to the systems we rely on. I expect I will work in this field for the rest of my life. And I'm more than okay with it.'

As we have seen, for this new generation of leaders, shareholder return and maximizing profits are not enough. They want to lead or be active participants in the social purpose of their companies – to contribute proactive solutions to help their companies meet their social responsibilities.

This aim – to shift the role of business from shareholder value to stakeholder value – is not new. Author and entrepreneur John Elkington created the triple bottom line business framework, focused on 'people,' planet and profit', in 1994.[45]

But I would add a fourth P, for purpose. Because a key driver behind the millennial and Generation Z approach to work is social purpose and purpose-driven leadership, some of which may be outside the broad issues of just climate or people.

Businesses that build a workplace culture around these ideals will be rewarded with highly engaged, enthusiastic, and invested employees. Many consultancies survey Millennials, but Deloitte's 10th anniversary survey research on Millennials suggests that 73 per cent of people working in a purpose-driven business are engaged.[46] With younger generations seeking purpose over pay, it's no wonder that companies with a focus on purpose outperform their competitors, having enhanced productivity levels with leaders who can get the best out of their people.

'I definitely recognize that my generation, Millennials, and the next set of younger generations, care more about social and environmental responsibility and are at the more passionate end when it comes to these issues,' says Venetia Bell of GIB Asset Management.

First they take these issues into account as consumers, with the brands they buy from, she says.[47]

'But as investors we invest in companies leading in their markets not only with profits, but also with issues around people and planet,' says Bell. 'As leaders, we want to lead companies that value profit, people, and planet. I am trying to persuade people that you can be environmentally and socially responsible and still make profits at the same time.'

Does this also apply to older managers and leaders, though?

'Most of the older Gen X group are somewhere between being converted and persuaded. But I think there is definitely a group between ages of 40 and 60 years old who are not quite with the program, they are more focused on what the bottom line is for the business.'

And this is potentially a problem for large organizations right now.

THE C-SUITE DECIDES

'Currently this middle generation of 40-60-year-olds are more in the C-level leadership positions where they make the decisions and allocate resources. And it is interesting that the leadership shift is starting to happen and Millennials are getting more into the leadership process. I am certain that more changes will come. Because there shouldn't be a trade-off between profits and purpose.'

Who else supports this?

'The silver generation, retirees, are becoming a lot more supportive. I get the impression that now they have made their money, they can afford to think about philanthropy and changing the world,' she says.

So pension holders and retirees from above, as well as the next generation of consumers and investors from below, are putting increasing pressure on corporations to make meaningful contributions to solving greater societal and environmental challenges. Combined with the internal pressures from the New Leaders of Change, the future looks hopeful.

New Leaders of Change are not only driving companies to have a higher social purpose, they are also demanding accountability, metrics, and authenticity. They want proof that companies and leaders are committed, that they are walking the talk. In today's world of fake news, lack of transparency, and the so-called green-washing of marketing practices, this generation values authenticity, transparency, and honesty.

In addition, many new stakeholders – including recruits to the leadership team and investors – will assess this commitment by whether companies incorporate Environmental, Social, and Governance (ESG) considerations into their management and investment portfolio decisions. Because companies will need to embed ESG goals firmly at the core of their strategy, rather than add them as an afterthought.

There are many examples of companies that continue to push forward their ESG agenda. Oil group Total, for example, has committed to net-zero emissions by 2050 following investor pressure, demonstrating how mitigating climate change is core to its business purpose.[48]

Beyond ESG, the UN's Sustainable Development Goals (SDG) are also a touchstone for the New Leaders of Change.

'Our vision as a business is to scale and mobilize capital in support of sustainable development,' says Venetia Bell. The firm invests in both conventional and Islamic assets and uses five pillars in its investment analysis that are directly derived from the UN's Sustainable Development Goals:

- Equality, diversity, and human capital development;
- Climate, environmental action, and water;
- Health and wellbeing;
- Governance and accountability;
- Innovation and infrastructure.

Bell says GIB is keen to work with partners to encourage the adoption of the SDGs across the Islamic finance universe. 'We already work with other asset owners and managers to improve outcomes through our active engagement approach on our investment portfolios, and find that joining with others allows a louder voice and greater momentum for positive change.'

So it's no surprise that new-generation investors themselves are making positive changes by putting direct pressure on firms. Anne-Sophie d'Andlau and Catherine Berjal founded their asset management firm CIAM (Charity Investment Asset Management) to bring about changes in corporate governance as well as help provide funds for charities. CIAM donates 25 per cent of its annual performance fees to charities dedicated to improving children's health and education across the world.

But the group's main impact is felt when they invest in a company and then demand changes in management, stakeholder transparency, adjustment of incentive structures, and board and governance.

Berjal and d'Andlau have been at the center of some of Europe's biggest corporate battles in recent years, including a bitter dispute with Walt Disney over its treatment of minority shareholders in Euro Disney and a successful campaign against Dutch retail giant Ahold Delhaize over its corporate governance shareholder engagement, transparency, and rights.

'The most common issues for poor corporate performance come from poor corporate governance and conflict of interest,' says d'Andlau. 'Without accountability to stakeholders, it creates a high concentration of power in a small group of people (the board), and/or one man or woman.'

Following pressure from the duo, French reinsurance group Scor is splitting the roles of Chief Executive and Chairman and establishing a clear succession plan, as long-serving CEO Denis Kessler steps down.[49] CIAM, which holds about 1 per cent of Scor, had outlined areas of 'significant concern'.

Berjal also wrote to Scor's shareholders raising concerns over Scor's ESG policy. 'For a company operating in the financial services sector, the level of sophistication on the Environmental, Social, and Governance (ESG) criteria incorporated within the bonus plan is worrying,' she wrote. 'There is no clear forward-looking quantitative ESG priorities set for 2020.'

Anne-Sophie d'Andlau is hopeful that big corporations and their shareholders are evolving and paying more attention to ESG issues. 'In the world of finance, ESG is the token that will make change go faster,' she says. 'There is more and more capital being dedicated to ESG topics and will eventually increase power of stakeholders, shareholders, and investors where we can drive and push for changes.'

This is why she is so excited about ESG.

'It is not a trend,' she says. 'It is going to make this all move faster. For example, a few years ago it was super-difficult to engage other shareholders. The big institutional shareholders would listen to us and then nothing would happen for two to three years. Today, it is much easier to engage them and have a constructive dialog and sometimes they even share our views and support us at the Annual General Meetings.'

Perhaps the idea of activist investors is much more common now?

'I believe it is becoming less taboo and more acceptable to express an opinion on ESG matters to these big asset managers. We are not there yet and the journey is still long, but there has been an evolution in the last couple years. I am hopeful that this trend will continue. There is more money coming into the ESG space in Europe and changes will accelerate.'

Bigger financial institutions and their older-generation bosses are beginning to agree. David Solomon, chairman and CEO of Goldman Sachs, has announced the firm would mobilize $750bn over a decade to address climate transition and inclusive growth.

In an opinion piece in the *Financial Times*, Solomon wrote, 'The needs of our clients will increasingly be defined by sustainable growth. Our firm's long term financial success, the stability of the global economy and society's overall wellbeing all depend on it.'[50]

Another activist investor is Katie Koch of Goldman Sachs Asset Management, whose investment team oversees about $60bn in assets globally. Their focus isn't exclusively ESG, though. She says GSAM plans to push companies for broader disclosure surrounding diversity, including people of color. While companies need to disclose the gender composition on their boards, they are not required to share data on other areas of diversity.

'If the treatment of people is diverse, inclusive, empowering, that's good for the employees and stakeholders,' Koch says. 'And if it's the opposite, and it can be exploitative, that's going to be bad long term.' The important thing is to keep the transformation moving in a positive direction, for the largest number of people.

Of course, transformational change towards a sustainable future means different things for different organizations, both for-profit and not-for-profit, and even for different industries and governments. What is increasingly clear, however, is that the New Leaders of Change will respond as individuals, as team leaders, and as business leaders in bold and inspiring ways that we can't even conceive yet. But in ways that will ultimately serve their business interests as much as the people they serve, as well as our society as a whole and the environment we all share.

That being said, the change and transformation process we face in this, the most advanced of all centuries, is only just beginning. Everything is in a state of motion. Everything is changing.

And if my father were here with me now, he would completely understand this.

'Everything changes,' he said after his trip to Uzbekistan all those years ago, looking for the past.

It's a message I will share with my granddaughter, to whom this book is dedicated. In the hope that she can shape her future however she wants to. When the time comes. ■

“Every now and then I have to come back to my center and remind myself of my mission and what brought me to this work in the first place. It is to ensure people and societies can be ready and resilient in the face of new threats to the systems we rely on.

Andrea Ruotolo
Senior Director
Liberty Utilities

Chapter 10

TOWARD PEOPLE-CENTERED LEADERSHIP

How the New Leaders of Change are changing themselves, their businesses, and the world

It was close to the end of the research phase for this book when I realized a number of pressing things were emerging. Importantly, while all the individual leaders I spoke to were unique in terms of their experiences and abilities, they also shared a number of significant characteristics and I'll come to those in a moment.

But first it's worth highlighting what this research means from an organizational perspective. Because the Fourth Industrial Revolution, and the exponential technologies it has given birth to, open up a new world of possibilities and competitive advantage for businesses. Let's be clear: the new sources of differentiation, value creation, innovation, and productivity are not lost on executives. However, not every company is prepared to handle the rapid pace of change, innovation, and opportunity that the revolution demands. What is not in doubt is that the organizations that cling to the traditional and linear, top-down hierarchy – designed for efficiency and predictability in an older industrial age – will fall behind in today's new disruptive economy. So to succeed in this new landscape, organizations must be designed above all for the agility, flexibility, adaptability, speed, and collaboration that are enabled by digital technologies. And that's a huge mountain to climb.

But there is an even greater challenge. Do firms have the right leaders in place to lead this type of digital and agile transformation? Because at the heart of the transformational challenge facing every organization are its leaders. And that's why there is such an urgency – organizations must understand the characteristics, competencies, and skills required of all its leaders to succeed. Getting this right should be your mission critical priority and here's where my research into the New Leaders of Change can help.

From the research underpinning this book over the past two years I've identified seven characteristics that are key to successful leadership in the 21st century. I've called them the Seven Cs of People-Centered Leadership (see Figure 1). It's important to note that the Seven Cs of People-Centered Leadership are not composed of skills or competencies – though there are aspects of the Seven Cs that can be learned and practiced. The Cs are characteristics and they're derived from the characters of the New Leaders of Change.

DEVELOPING THE SEVEN Cs MODEL

What you'll realize by now is that the leaders in this book all embraced adversity and challenge. They had the courage to take a leap into the unknown, whether it was a new job, a new country, or an apparently impossible task. And studying their journey in-depth, something profound struck me: it became evident that in the midst of not-knowing what to do next, and facing their challenges head-on, they were able to get in touch with and strengthen their inner selves and their unique characteristics – what it was that made them who they were. Characteristics such as courage, compassion, and conviction were built through their direct experiences of success, failure, and internal conflict. It's significant, I feel, that these experiences weren't built in classroom settings. You'll also recognize from the modest nature of the stories they told me about themselves that the interviewees who were a part of this study were not always born with these qualities.

In short, I realized that what these leaders exemplified was the power of knowing your purpose, recognizing the opportunity that is aligned with your purpose, and then – with conviction – taking a leap, and making a commitment to the journey. These are strong themes for us as individuals, especially as we live in times of constant disruption and constant rapid change.

What I also found hugely exciting was that these leaders did not dwell on the moments of crisis, fear, and adversity. Instead they viewed these experiences as opportunities to learn and grow, in large part by reaching out to a network of people who provided the support and encouragement they needed. And this is another strong theme we're seeing now: the shift away from individual expertise towards collective wisdom and the intelligence of ecosystems.

But as I have listened to the stories of the leaders in this book, I can also share that clearly it was not always easy to lead well. The same will be true for you. Sometimes it will take all your courage and conviction to stay true to your purpose and to take on that next challenge. Because you will always have questions. How will you know when to be courageous, and fight for what you believe in, and when to have the humility to accept what is given? How will you know when to act with the conviction that you're right and when should you admit that you just don't know what action to take? There are high stakes all around.

Unfortunately I can't help you with specifics. But another lesson from the New Leaders of Change could be useful here: the practice of taking a moment to pause and reflect. Because to be aware of your own thoughts and reflections is always a good place to start. As well as being aware of what others are thinking and feeling, and the context in which you are working. Taking this moment for yourself can help you understand the source of your emotional reactions, and the reactions of others in a given context. It will give you a moment of clarity.

How can I say this? Well, the leaders in this book have well developed emotional intelligence and almost all of them practice some form of mindfulness to build their self-awareness muscle. And self-awareness is a key to connecting with your purpose when leadership is hard and when the choices are not clear-cut. It can help you put your ego aside. To realize that to steer the journey towards your purpose and inspire and mobilize the team, you need to go deep inside yourself. Only then will you find the courage you need to act. Only then will you develop the commitment to your purpose or the conviction to be a catalyst for change.

Putting this all together for readers of this book, I hope you feel reassured. The overarching conclusion is that while leaders come in many shapes and sizes – and you each have a unique journey, of course – the characteristics of these New Leaders of Change remain broadly the same. Of course, how you develop and deploy those characteristics will differ – depending on who you are and the particular context facing you in your organization. My hope for the book is that no matter where you are on your leadership journey, you will be able to learn something about yourself, how you lead, your strengths and weaknesses, and that you will be inspired to continually learn and grow.

INTRODUCING THE SEVEN Cs OF PEOPLE-CENTERED LEADERSHIP

The Seven Cs of People-Centered Leadership, then, are these:

- Connectedness
- Conviction
- Collaboration
- Compassion
- Curiosity
- Change catalyst
- Courage

Figure 1: The Seven Cs of People-Centered Leadership

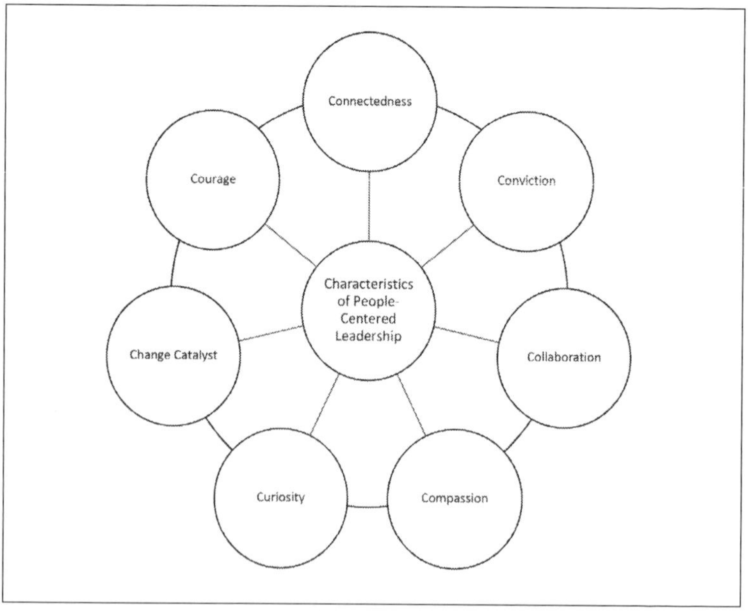

As business landscapes become increasingly networked and distributed, and as the new generation of leaders enter the workforce, there is a natural movement away from hierarchical leadership models in favor of these seven C leadership approaches. And when these seven leadership characteristics combine, something magical happens. Each feeds the others, creating a virtuous interconnected web of characteristics. If you can identify the characteristics in which you are strongest and begin to enhance the characteristics that don't come so naturally, it will help you change the way you lead forever.

I'll summarize the lessons from the research here and highlight some of the exemplars that help define the seven characteristics.

CONNECTEDNESS

From Individualism to Connectedness

Connections are everywhere: enterprises are hyper-connected, society is networked, groups of businesses are ecosystems, our approach is always multistakeholder. In other words we are talking of a new business paradigm where people are truly connected to information, things, our environments, and above all to each other. What this means is we need to move beyond the transactional nature of relationships – with employees, customers, and partners – to unleash the transformative power of deep human connection. This is not about the technologies that enable hyperconnectivity. This is about having connected leaders who can orchestrate large-scale collaborations and catalyze the change we need. (See *Table 5, The Four Levels of Connected Leadership.*)

And the leaders in this study – Linda Dörig, Martin Baart, and Andrea Ruotolo, for example – certainly do have highly developed levels of awareness. So much so that their sense of connection has influenced the trajectory of their entire professional careers. Other connected leaders – such as Adrian Locher at Merantix, among others – seek to deepen relationships with people by being authentic and accessible, trustworthy, and transparent. This is in addition to and perhaps beyond their ability to embrace digital and new forms of communication tools to connect with a broad ecosystem of people. Their ability to connect and develop meaningful relationships, or networks of diverse individuals, is hugely valuable. It creates personal and business resilience in the face of today's volatile, uncertain, complex, and ambiguous business context.

Table 6: The four levels of connected leadership[51, 52, 53]

Connected leadership is a new way of leading through people, relationships, influence, and engagement. Connected leadership requires four levels of awareness:

1. **Self Awareness:**
   a. Connected leaders are self-aware and have a connection with the deepest parts of themselves – their purpose, values, mindset, and underlying assumptions about what they believe. They understand that their social identity – their race, culture, gender, geography, socio-economic class, and education, for example – informs their understanding of power, privilege, and leadership.
   b. Self-awareness of our actions and their impact on other people enables us to change, grow, and expand our sense of personal identity, the things that define us as a person.
   c. As we increase our self-awareness we expand our attention to include the other three levels of awareness and our ability to see the interconnected nature of all things.

2. **Social-Relational Awareness:**
   a. The ability to understand and engage with people having multiple points of view and taking the perspective of those with different backgrounds. This informs your ability to cultivate empathy and express compassion.
   b. The ability to understand the socio-cultural, political, and historical context of individuals and groups when fostering collaboration, partnerships, and participation.

3. **Contextual or Systems Awareness:**
   a. Understanding the connections, tensions, and inter-dependencies between multiple systems often seen as separate and autonomous – for example, between corporations, the economy, labor, governments, education, health, environment, and communities.
   b. Connected leaders understand that today's wicked problems require inter-systemic change – not siloed solutions. They have the ability to examine critically the inter-systemic impacts of decisions and have an awareness of the unintended consequences of decisions.
   c. Contextual awareness requires leaders to understand systems dynamics, patterns, and relationships to leverage the power of the ecosystem to mobilize action and commitment.

4. **Planetary Awareness:**
   a. Having planetary awareness includes connectedness to the human and non-human world.
   b. Understanding and awareness that all living things are interconnected and interdependent through ecological systems.
   c. Understanding and taking responsibility for the impact of business on the communities in which it operates and on the environment.
   d. Making a commitment to environmentally sustainable practices to help build thriving communities and secure future growth.

Why does this matter? Well, in today's hyperconnected, digitally driven, accelerated, and information-intensive society, the human connection is the new competitive advantage for businesses everywhere. Because whatever value you create in your business is likely to come from your relationship with another human being.

So continue to build your connectedness. It matters.

CONVICTION

From Uncertainty and Ambiguity to Conviction

One of the superpowers of the leaders in this study is their deeply held conviction. It almost always starts with their strong sense of collective purpose – which is often their organization's reason for being. It is the 'reason why' behind so many specific decisions and actions they take. Building on this is their confidence in people, which grounds them in the philosophy that 'we' rather than 'I' are the ones that will succeed.

Leaders with conviction – people including Anne-Sophie d'Andlau of CIAM and Christy Lake of Twilio as exemplars – are incredibly valuable in a fast-changing business environment. These times are so often full of uncertainty and offer no clear roadmap or playbook for how to lead. It's a situation made more complex by our human brains, wired to respond to uncertainty with fear and anxiety. We are secretly preoccupied to bring back certainty and normality. This utterly human reaction tends to make people less effective, productive, and resilient.

You can see why creating an environment of certainty and optimism, with a bias for action toward the collective vision, is so essential. It creates a feeling that we are all headed in the right direction, that together we will succeed. Perhaps even more importantly it suggests that our future together is certain.

In analyzing these results for this book I've discovered that something else happens, too. Because when you become convinced – as an authentic leader – that a new, different future is possible, it leads inevitably to your curiosity and creativity, and the courage to try new solutions. Which is exactly what teams and businesses need at times like these and they in turn become energized.

The web of these seven characteristics and their impact on each other is uncanny. But perhaps it all starts here, with conviction. It prompts me to ask you, before we go any further, what are your convictions?

What do you stand for? What or who would you make sacrifices for?

COLLABORATION

From Hierarchy & Authority to Collaboration

When we explored connected leaders earlier, I suggested that collaborative leadership was a natural outcome for leading effectively inside the organization. In fact, it seems to help us to lead across the ecosystem of all our stakeholders: from customers and investors to partners and communities. This has been such a striking revelation, in countless stories from my interviewees, that I reach a new conclusion: that perhaps the drive to influence and inspire through collaboration on its own is enough to separate the new generation of leaders from more traditional leaders – those trying to control their organizations by exercising positional power.

What does collaborative leadership look like, then? Well, we tend to see a great deal of coaching, supporting, and empowering rather than controlling and micromanaging. Consider leaders such as Venetia Bell, formerly with the Bank of England, Katie Koch, of Goldman Sachs Asset Management, and Paulo Pontin, Managing Partner, Latin America at Verizon Enterprise Solutions; they seek out diverse opinions and ideas from their employees, and they create an inclusive environment. As a result, employees are more engaged, they feel trusted, and they're energized. Importantly, they are encouraged to create, contribute, and share ideas without a formal hierarchy or chain of command. That's in contrast to the traditional top-down organizational models of leadership, where only a small group of executives controls the flow of information.

Together the collaborative culture and open communications enable employees to exchange ideas across organizational boundaries. They create a culture where anyone is able to talk to anyone else, at any level, at any time – and without fear of retribution or humiliation. Collaborative leaders seem to be able to create psychologically safe spaces in which to work. They are great enablers.

In addition, collaborative leaders keep communication lines open and engage in purposeful conversations far beyond the boundaries of their organizations. As a result they create wide coalitions and can harvest the community's collective intelligence to solve unusual challenges

– those that are large and complex. The ones we face every day.

In part it seems to be empathy that fuels collaboration. Those leaders high in emotional intelligence can identify, understand, and navigate tension and conflict, which they don't see as unpleasant or destructive. Instead they see it as a force for innovation, creativity, and positive change, and once again we can see the web of connections between these different characteristics. Don't get me wrong: collaborative leadership isn't a quick fix. It takes time to develop a culture of psychological safety and trust, but small actions can add up to a big impact over time. Start now.

COMPASSION

From Indifference to Compassionate Leadership

Compassionate leaders such as Felicia Würtenberger at Flooz, Banks Baker at Google, and Donna See, CEO at Xora Innovation, are self-aware and mindful. They pay attention to their own feelings and thoughts. But they are also keenly aware of the impact they have on others and are attentive to the needs of others. They take action when faced with employees who are in a difficult situation, or when they see suffering and pain. They have awareness and understanding of the emotional state of other people and can seem to read what other people are thinking and feeling. Empathy is a skill that enables us to connect with other people, which can lead us to feel compassion toward them. Compassionate leadership, in return, increases the likelihood of collaboration, trust, and loyalty from the team.

Why is this important? Some leaders continue to think that business is business and compassion has no place there. But compassion is a fundamental virtue inherent in human existence and it's rooted in a basic human need – the need to care and help others.

I remember a graduation speech given by Jeff Weiner, former CEO of LinkedIn, at Wharton Business School a few years ago.[54] 'Compassion is putting yourself in the shoes of another person,' he said, 'and seeing the world through their lens for the sake of alleviating their suffering.' In other words, compassion is empathy plus action.

Then he said something that stuck with me. 'I can tell you with absolute conviction that managing compassionately is not just a better way to build a team: it's a better way to build a company.' It's an inspiring thought.

CURIOSITY

From Fixed Mindset to Curiosity

By now it should be clear that none of the characteristics of people-centered leaders is a stand-alone trait or skill. Curiosity in particular is a higher order meta-skill, infused through the other six leadership characteristics, enabling and magnifying them all. Curiosity enables creativity, for instance, a gateway to exploration and innovation. It is about setting sail on voyages beyond the map of the known, challenging our long-held beliefs and assumptions, and allowing ourselves to be surprised.

Curious leaders such as Andrea Buetler of Worley and Linda Dörig of Gebana are explorers in this vein. They show an endless desire to learn or know more about the world, whether that means things, processes or people. This is important because a willingness to explore what you don't know is the foundation for leading with modesty and humility, and actually it's an important key to leading more effectively in the 21st century.

When curious leaders face complex challenges, for example, they reveal their beginner's mind. They continually ask relevant, strategic, thoughtful, and targeted questions, asking questions without assumptions – questions such as 'why', 'how' and 'what if'. And being able to ask different questions opens our minds, connecting us to each other. This stretches the thinking of all of us and keeps us learning.

What does this achieve? First, it creates the space for curiosity and sparks creativity, and that in turn inspires new ways of looking at problems. It opens the door to a wider range of possibilities. It's this that equips us to manage complexity and ambiguity.

Partly this is because curious leaders understand there is huge value in taking perspectives that are conflicting, opposing or just plain annoying. Perhaps they take up perspectives most people don't even notice. Whatever perspectives they consider, you can be sure they create the right conditions for constructive discussion, helping everyone to reflect, learn, and innovate.

CHANGE CATALYST

From Managing Change to Being a Catalyst for Change

Leaders who are catalysts for change, such as Banks Baker at Google and Thomas Klein at Jodel, inspire and lead people toward a vision for a better future with agility, empathy, and shared purpose. They take tough decisions, calculated risks, and bold actions in the face of uncertainty and disruption. A key attribute of the change catalyst is that ability they have to step into a situation where the future is uncertain, information is incomplete, and data are conflicting. Then they create clarity for the people they're leading, they speed up the change process and spark action by mobilizing people.

Significantly, they know that every step along the change journey requires deep human-to-human connection. They understand that they must demonstrate the human values of authenticity, empathy, compassion, and trust. Because they need to keep people – all their key stakeholders – front and center at all costs. They understand that people are at the core of change and that they need to be part of the process of designing and implementing the change that they face.

Importantly, change catalysts can harness collective performance, resilience, and intelligence from multiple teams, networks, and ecosystems. And they recognize the value of continuous growth and learning. For themselves, their teams, and their organizations.

Finally in this section it's worth saying that change catalysts can emerge from any level in the organizations and that their leadership isn't about power over others; it's about being the change they wish to see in the world.

COURAGE

From Fear of Failing to Courage to take Bold Action

Courageous leaders, such as Trevor Campbell at Tapjoy and Nirupa Chander of Hitachi Energy, have a clear sense of purpose and are prepared to stand up for what they believe in. They take bold action without knowing whether it's going to be successful, they let go of fear, and they let go of worrying about being judged, criticized, or liked.

A particular strength of courageous leaders is they understand the importance of action in a complex world. So they engage in rapid iteration, they experiment, they assess progress, and they act again. The upshot is that courageous leaders can bring their ideas to life quickly.

Courageous leaders also speak up on controversial topics and aim to move paralyzing discussions to decision and action. And they are willing to take personal accountability for unpopular decisions.

Above all, courageous leaders know that change, transformation, and innovation require thinking big, disrupting the *status quo* to introduce ground-breaking tools, and tradition-defying ways of operating differently.

However, it is important to understand that although courageous leadership comes in many shapes and forms, it is not about heroes or heroism. It can simply be, for example, about examining and understanding your own beliefs and assumptions, and then having the courage to change your own mindset and behaviors. For others, it might be challenging the *status quo* in more creative ways such as making art, or writing a book.

Some leaders may be engaged in a deep change of their organizations, helping everyone to re-evaluate deeply held beliefs and behaviors. Or they could be redesigning an organization's systems, processes, and ways of working for the benefit of people, the planet, and profit. That takes courage.

For others still, it might be protesting or marching, having their voice heard among a community of people for a shared purpose. Leading with courage is not necessarily a one-person band, a single heroic leader.

This is significant because there is a strong belief that today's global issues are too complex to be solved by single individuals, single institutions, and even single countries. So we need to let go of what could be called a narcissistic heroic courage and to embrace collective leadership courage. We need to harness the courage of coalitions and alliances from very diverse group of communities.

REFLECTING ON THE 7Cs OF PEOPLE-CENTERED LEADERSHIP

The seven Cs of people-centered leadership is a tool for self-reflection, but also for self-development. When I interviewed the new-generation leaders for this book, they all either expressed these qualities naturally, or they had to think about them outside of their education and their work experience. As a result, some of them created experiences for themselves, outside of work as well as inside the work environment, to develop their own skills and experience. Or somebody else's, if they were in a developmental role.

So what tends to happen, and this is what I encourage, is thinking about yourself and your leadership in a more mindful way. In the same way someone would develop their technical or professional skills, the next-generation leaders may need to develop themselves as people-centered leaders. (And I stress may need to develop.) But I really don't want to make this complicated. Sometimes it's just a slight shift in your focus and mindset. And that's what the 7Cs model does – it just makes all the elements of people-centered leadership visible.

And above all, it has to be said, there is something in people-centered leaders about commitment. So let me ask you now: how committed are you to this journey? Do you truly care about people? Do you truly care about your team members or your employees or your business partners?

Next time you see them, will you look in their eyes and ask: how is it going? How are your kids? How did you cope in this last year? Because I think people-centered leaders are not afraid to ask questions like that.

Maybe it's just a small shift in your focus initially, which might give you the courage to share more, to ask more questions. And maybe that's enough to help you become more committed, to get to know people even better than you already do.

FROM CHARACTERISTICS TO ARCHETYPES
The Archetypes of People-Centered Leadership

In researching the amazing men and women who make up the backbone of this book, I became aware that they shared very different characteristics, behaviors, and skills. But I also noticed there were clusters of people who shared similar characteristics. So I dug deeper and have now codified these characteristics into a series of archetypes which emerged from the research.

We're familiar with archetypes from the world of storytelling and we see them in literature, film, and theater. When a group of personalities seems to share similar patterns, characteristics, and behaviors they're described as an archetype. That's not to say they are stereotypes or labels, an overly simplified, generalized, and exaggerated set of character traits. An archetype is a set of patterns and a base to build upon and what I've seen in this research is that leadership characteristics, patterns, and behaviors can coalesce in the same way. Whether that's making sure your employees' development and well-being are the priority, innovating the next successful business model, or successfully transforming a dying company.

Before we get into the different archetypes, and you start to identify which group most resonates with you, there are some things I need to say. First, there is no right or wrong archetype. You are likely to display more characteristics of one archetype than another and that's okay. But that raises another question. How can people-centered leaders differ so widely?

The way I look at this is that, despite differences in characteristics, personalities, motivations, and inspirations, people-centered leaders share a common humanistic philosophy, a belief system that guides their decisions and behaviors. They lead by humane principles, values, and perspectives. For example, an entrepreneur leader – and I'll share what that looks like in a moment – will have a very different approach, principles, and aspirations depending on if they prescribe to humanistic philosophy and principles or to Machiavellianism.

People-centered entrepreneurs on the one hand would engage key stakeholders that are important – customers, partners, employees, investors, and others – to increase collaboration, trust, and mutual benefit to make their vision a reality. A Machiavellian entrepreneur might still engage multiple stakeholders, but they would undertake this very differently. He or she would focus on how to manipulate stakeholders and to use whatever proved necessary to bring their vision to reality, gaining political or personal power along the way.

HOW ARE THE CHARACTERISTICS AND THE ARCHETYPES CONNECTED?

First, I want to point out that while the following archetypes are distinctive, the archetypes share a set of core values. Because they all represent individuals who are people-centric. You can't be a servant leader or a socially conscious leader or a visionary leader unless you're people-centric. I just want to make that clear.

In other words, the New Leaders of Change share all of the seven C characteristics. But some characteristics are more obvious than others in the way those leaders behave. And it's these differences in how they deploy the characteristics of human-centered leadership that show up in the form of the different archetypes.

In Table 7 you can see a summary of which archetypes most demonstrate which characteristics.

THE VISIONARY LEADER

Exemplar of curiosity, courage, conviction, and change catalyst

The Visionary Leaders in this study are innovative and appear to be able to see the future, perhaps by inferring from barely visible trends, and they create markets where none existed previously. They seem to push the boundaries of what's possible.

With their sense of purpose, potential, and possibility, Visionary Leaders can be inspiring. They dare to envision a better future which they pursue with passion and conviction. In fact, it's their radical conviction, courage, and dedication that inspire others to believe in and pursue the vision, too.

Their visionary thinking may sometimes come across as lofty or disruptive, and to others who don't think like them they may seem out of touch with reality. But they are not afraid to go against the *status quo* and they pride themselves in their originality and out-of-the-box thinking.

As well as almost seeing the future, Visionary Leaders are strategic thinkers who can translate a vision into a strategy, highlighting the direction of travel and offering some sense of destination. They are people of action who will tenaciously pursue their vision as long-term thinkers with a sense of urgency.

During times of uncertainty and rapid change, visionary leadership is more vital than ever. Because the Visionary Leader embraces chaos and uncertainty and often sees them as an opportunity. Their clarity around the future often provides a sense of stability, optimism, and a North Star for their teams.

In fact as well as leading their teams, Visionary Leaders can mobilize organizations, shareholders, and whole industries. They can help colleagues and employees to challenge their assumptions about old ways of working, and help them connect their jobs to the vision, purpose, and strategy of the organization.

Table 7: How the characteristics of people-centered leadership come to life in the archetypes

	Visionary Leader	Entrepreneurial Leader	Servant Leader	Socially Conscious Leader	Emergent Leader
Connectedness		●	●	●	●
Conviction	●	●	●	●	●
Collaboration					
Compassion			●	●	
Curiosity	●	●			
Change Catalyst	●		●	●	●
Courage	●	●			●

THE ENTREPRENEURIAL LEADER

Exemplar of curiosity, courage, conviction, and connection

Like entrepreneurs themselves, the Entrepreneurial Leaders in this research take risks, discover opportunities, and create new paths. They offer a bold vision for new ventures, new businesses, and new industries.

Successful Entrepreneurial Leaders display a deep sense of curiosity that allows them continuously to seek new opportunities, create new paths and explore different avenues. They have intensely inquisitive minds. They continuously ask questions, challenge the *status quo*, and proactively attack challenges rather than avoid them.

As they explore new approaches and new paths they lead with a conviction that allows them and the organizations they lead to weather the inevitable storms and to stay on track. They are by nature connectors of people and have strong networks. So, they work hard to foster a culture of enthusiasm, deep connection, belonging, high engagement, and mutual purpose.

What's striking about the Entrepreneurial Leader in comparison with the Visionary Leader, say, is how customer and market obsessed they are. They spend a lot of time in the process of research and discovery, most often in close collaboration with customers, partners, investors, advisors, and other communities.

What makes Entrepreneurial Leaders unique, perhaps, is their level of persistence. They persevere when the going gets tough and appear to thrive in a context that is risky, complex, and uncertain. They see failures as opportunities to learn, grow, and try again. The possibility of success drives them forward.

However, with their bias for action they can sometimes move too fast with too much conviction and passion, which can be detrimental to their long-term success.

THE SERVANT LEADER

Exemplar of compassion, connection, conviction, and change catalyst

Servant leaders in the 21st century focus primarily on the growth, development, and well-being of people in ways that radically unlock their potential, creativity, and sense of purpose. Servant Leaders believe that when you create motivated, engaged, and high-performing employees, you will meet and often exceed customer or shareholder expectations. But make no mistake, servant leaders are results-driven. They understand that they are ultimately responsible for the success of their employees and the success of their business.

One of the key tenets of servant leadership is the sharing of power when it comes to team decisions. Instead of making decisions on what is best for the team, Servant Leaders empower the team to take the decision by sharing relevant information and data. They do this because they don't think of themselves as bosses. Instead they see their roles as stewards, guiding the ship while focusing on the well-being of their people. That includes taking care of the resources that teams need to be successful, by the way. They lead by influence, inspiration, and empowerment and create a positive environment that allows people to take on challenges, learn, and perform to the best of their ability.

It's no surprise that Servant Leaders make sure to form a culture that emphasizes inclusivity, collaboration, and trust, which leads to more and better teamwork, deeper engagement, and ultimately better results and success. And perhaps, beyond everything, it's the Servant Leader's authenticity, empathy, and compassion that create the emotional and psychological safety that employees need to excel at their jobs and deliver value to customers and shareholders.

THE SOCIALLY CONSCIOUS LEADER

Exemplar of compassion, connection, change catalyst, and conviction

The research background underpinning Socially Conscious Leaders links a number of the big ideas we have been discussing so far. First, the Socially Conscious Leaders in this study are aware of the interconnectedness of life, respecting cultural diversity and human rights, advocating social justice and greater equality, for example. They empathize with suffering people around the globe. Secondly, Socially Conscious Leaders feel a deep regard if not a moral responsibility for the planet. And thirdly, as business leaders, they believe that companies should have a higher purpose than focusing solely on profit. Don't get me wrong – they also understand that businesses need profits to exist and to strive towards their socially conscious purpose.

Importantly, Socially Conscious Leaders consider what you might call societal initiatives as fundamental to their businesses. They are ambitious in addressing them and are driven to demonstrate success in doing well by doing good. Indeed, they are committed to generating new and profitable revenue streams through socially or environmentally conscious products or services. It could be said, then, that they strive to be a catalyst for change above all, driving for change at the organizational, governmental, and societal levels. They do this in part by examining their organizational culture and processes, their operations and governance, and their impact on society and the environment. In short, Socially Conscious Leaders tend to think holistically and systemically, to understand the interconnected relationships between business, society, and the natural world.

Finally, as well as focusing on global level issues, Socially Conscious Leaders understand the power of doing the inner work of self-awareness and reflection, enhancing their abilities to be more empathetic and compassionate in the future.

THE EMERGENT LEADER

Exemplar of courage, change catalyst, conviction, and connection

The concept of emergent leadership, derived from the exemplars in this research, can be summed up like this: it's leadership which doesn't come from any formal position or power, but rather it emerges from an individual's initiative and their commitment to step up to a challenging situation. The emergence of leadership is a social process, where key individuals become recognized as leaders by their peers within their organization, community or team.

What's clear is that Emergent Leaders are less focused on positions, power, and self-interest for themselves. They are, however, tightly focused on the shared purpose and goals of the community. They're also very concerned with how to harness the collective intelligence, experience, and consciousness of the community to respond to the current challenges. And they do this to co-create community-based solutions.

Emergent Leaders seem to thrive in environments of change and uncertainty, and even in situations of crisis. They are socially connected and are able to listen deeply with empathy, and they lead by example and with authenticity.

Importantly, Emergent Leaders tend to be politically savvy. They know when and where to push, or where to pull, and by how much. And they tend to be natural mentors, coaches, and sponsors, often bringing out the best in people and making them, in turn, Emergent Leaders.

NEXT STEPS?

Why build these archetypes out of my research? How do they help you? And having explored the individual archetypes, how can you use them to help your own future development?

Well, I've summarized some of my thoughts in Table 8, but let me say here that it's important not just to put yourself or your people in boxes. You can, however, use the Seven Cs and the archetypes I'm sharing with you as tools to really understand what drives, motivates, and inspires you and your leaders. I want you to really acknowledge, to know, and understand... who is this person? What drives them? How can I, as the leader, or a consultant, or as a leadership development person, how can I put them in places where they can thrive and be the best version of themselves? Because that's the way you or they are going to add the most value to the organization.

Let's take an example. Because as I've said if you deeply understand what drives and inspires you as a person, you can then take up positions where you can thrive, lead, and inspire, like a Servant Leader, for example. Servant Leaders are really precious leaders, by the way, because they love to serve and above all they love people. They want to make individuals as well as teams successful. They are a great asset to an organization. But they are not the only asset.

This process of reviewing these archetypes is also valuable if you're responsible for your talent pipeline. Understanding the archetypes in this tool, you can better place people in positions where they can thrive – but only if you truly understand the nuances of people-centered leadership.

I think there's a challenge for all of us, in some ways, because we often don't know the kind of leader we are. In my interviews many if not most of the people I talked to didn't understand why they were so successful. Or why, sometimes, the things they tried actually didn't work. And it all goes back to understanding yourself.

So have a look through these different archetypes – one of them will have some resonance for you, or maybe two. Look closely at the descriptions of those archetypes, and get a feel for what it is that excites you most in the text. And then seek out more of those experiences, more of that work. This will definitely give you an insight into the kind of roles

Table 8: How to use the archetypes of people-centered leadership [55]

The Young Leader
Well, let's say you are a young leader developing your leadership philosophy, character, and skills. As part of your leadership journey you can use the people-centered leadership principles, characteristics, and archetypes as another set of tools for building your self-awareness. Who are you? What motivates your choices when it comes to action? And what is your purpose?

The Seasoned Leader
If you're a seasoned leader and you believe your personal leadership development process is never truly finished, maybe you realize the world is changing exponentially and the leadership approach and skills that worked for you in the past are not as effective in the present. Or perhaps you realize the feedback from your new generation of employees does not align with how you perceive your own leadership. These characteristics and archetypes of people-centered leadership can provide you with a different perspective from which to reflect and ask different questions. For example, what drives you forward in your leadership journey? What aspects of your purpose and core values need to change for today's leadership challenges and context? What ultimately matters to you?

The Leadership Development Professional
Finally, if you're a leadership coach, or you're in charge of leadership development or talent management in your organization, you probably know that the need for leadership development has never been more urgent. Indeed your stakeholders themselves – leaders from diverse industries and organizations – realize that to survive in today's business environment, they need different leadership skills and organizational capabilities from those that helped them succeed in the past. And it isn't just you seeing this.

The annual leadership development survey conducted by *Training* magazine in the USA saw an increased interest in developing leadership character in many areas we've been discussing: connectedness and belonging; curiosity and creativity; promoting diversity; resilience; and finally integrity, ethics, and trust. All of these issues directly address how leaders treat other people.

So see the principles, characteristics, and archetypes of people-centered leadership as a guide to help you think about how to curate leadership coaching and development programs to address today's challenges.

that you might want to undertake in the future.

Now, if you're already lucky enough to have recognized that you're on a journey to become even more focused on people-centered leadership, or if you're a manager responsible for actively seeking New Leaders of Change, then you can begin to look for people to fill the roles that you have. But in a much more detailed way than previously. In a much more detailed way than 'we're looking for a team leader, or a section head, or a CEO'.

Because there are these noticeable but subtle distinctions in the leaders you need in certain circumstances. And to develop a more mature, people-centered organization, you need to understand these refined and subtle differences, even more than we have in the past.

CONCLUSION

Towards People-Centered Leadership

Let's end by stating the obvious: there is no single kind of human-centered leader. It's possible, in fact, that there are many more types of human-centered leader than these models show. For us as individuals this is good news. As long as you demonstrate some of these characteristics, then you can make an increasing difference in the humanistic workplace of the 21st century.

Executives at the top of organizations might be less happy. Because they need to understand that they can't build a treadmill to create the same kind of leader over and over. It will require time, effort, and understanding, particularly in the early stages of the journey towards crafting an organization of human-centered leaders. They will need to create links between people who perhaps have never communicated or worked together before. But this effort and the associated costs will eventually pay off. The formal meetings and contacts will become informal relationships, and managers who work together on a taskforce will continue to message or phone each other naturally about the variety of day-to-day challenges and issues that they face.

Is human-centered leadership only for medium-to-large companies? No. Is it only for Western organizations? Emphatically, no. This book has focused on research with a range of people from all over the world, and in companies of all different sizes. And the new leadership concepts that have emerged provide a set of insights and a few tools you can use to think through what is changing around you. And I hope it's given you the impetus to build the kind of leadership you need to survive and succeed in the increasingly humanistic world of work.

Finally, I invite you to have the courage to ask different questions, to find new sources of inspiration, and to re-energize your ambition. Be open to a wider range of possibilities regarding your business, your leadership, and your relationships. It could be the start of a new journey. ■

The NEW LEADERS of CHANGE

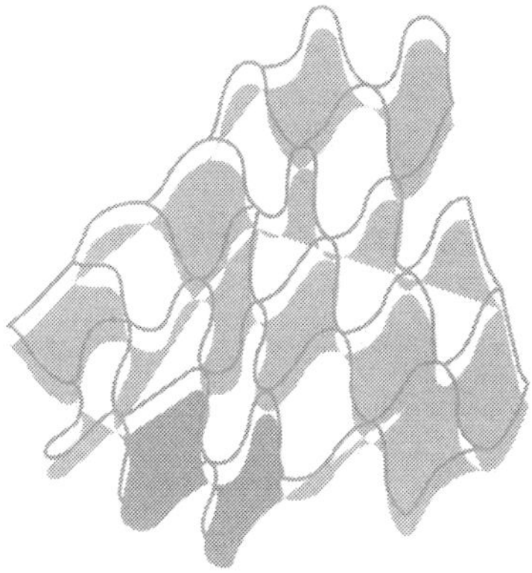

APPENDICES AND RESOURCES

Appendix A

HOW I RESEARCHED AND WROTE THIS BOOK

The research design and methodology

From the beginning I was very clear I wanted to co-write this book with the new generation of leaders, from their perspective. I decided on a simple design with three different research positions to organize my inquiry:

1. **Author's Lens**
My own perspective, experience, and reflections
My personal perspective and the choices I made throughout the research, analysis, and writing process. To aid this process I kept a journal of notes, reflections, and next steps throughout the research process.

2. **Community Lens**
Existing secondary research, discussions, and articles
A focus on the way other researchers, authors, and colleagues have constructed the experience of the new generation of leaders and leadership, as well as of change and transformation.

3. **Leader's Lens**
Wholly new primary research, including more than 50 semi-structured interviews focused on the lived experiences of next generation leaders
The research stance of this study can be loosely associated with the social constructionist grounded theory methodology. I set out to interview about 20 new generation leaders using a semi-structured interview protocol. In the end I interviewed just over 50 people from 11 countries together with researchers in the leadership area, colleagues in business and influencers in the personal development space.

When I approached the interviews, I adopted a beginner's mind, rather than the mindset of a change, transformation, and leadership expert with 25+ years of experience. I took a few moments before each interview to ensure my mindset was judgment-free and I was in a state of curiosity, openness, and being present.

I wanted to understand the complexities, nuances, and unique experience of each person I was interviewing. So I focused my attention on how the individuals made sense of their leadership journey and created meaning for themselves along that journey.

While conducting the interviews, I was fascinated by how an open inquiry of the interviewees' different viewpoints and experiences led to new ideas and concepts regarding change, transformation, and leadership. I came to appreciate how subjective, individual, relational, and personal each person's narrative about their leadership was.

The structure of the interviews enabled the interviewees to engage deeper with their own experience and meaning as a leader. Often after the interview was completed, they would comment that they not only enjoyed it, but also learned a lot about themselves as leaders.

One participant shared: 'I have never really thought about or considered many of the experiences I shared today as significant to my leadership style before.'

Another was grateful 'for the opportunity to reflect and learn about my leadership and how I came to develop myself as a leader'.

Often, these interviews went deep into the leaders' personal experiences, feelings, and thoughts, before shifting into reflection and theorizing about leadership, change, and transformation in a general way. This process facilitated the co-construction of patterns and narratives about leadership and change.

The interviews were conducted and recorded on the Zoom audio and video platform and first transcribed using the AI software platform Temi before being personally reviewed and edited by me, multiple times.

Data analysis – an iterative process

Analysis was an iterative process because of the vast amounts of data in the form of transcripts. These I read repeatedly, identified themes, evaluated the relationship of specific quotes and stories to the various themes, and examined the relationship of themes with each other.

As the purpose of my study was to construct a framework to understand the New Leaders of Change and how they undertook transformation, I used aspects of the grounded theory approach developed by the sociologists Barney Glaser and Anselm Strauss (Glaser and Strauss, 1970) to ensure that my conclusions and frameworks would be grounded in the rich data collected. I created a simple four-column table:

- First column: the original question;
- Second column: the evolving answers that emerged;
- Third column: my evolving interpretation of meanings;
- Fourth column: the key emergent themes, used to identify patterns in the transcripts.

Next I created another table and organized the data by themes. The chapters of the book emerged naturally from the common themes identified during the data analysis.

As I analyzed, structured, coded, and assigned pieces of data to certain themes, I simultaneously engaged with the existing research and my own experience and knowledge as a practitioner in change, transformation, and leadership. The majority of the existing literature I reviewed did not make it into the book; however, it informed my choices during data analysis and building the models.

Despite this, I was mindful to ensure that the analytical process was not constrained by existing scholarship or my own knowledge. I stayed true and close to the stories and narratives of the leaders I interviewed. I paid attention to several surprises in the data and expanded my own thinking and scope of the book to include those surprises.

A good example is Chapter 9, Changing the World: A purpose beyond business. In my original book plan, there was no chapter on environmental concerns and sustainability. However, the voices of the new generation of leaders spoke very loudly, and I had to not only include a chapter on it but also do a deep-dive on the subject for my own learning.

This book does not provide a precise description of what it means to be a 'new generation leader'. Rather, this book presents a cohesive narrative that emerged from the shared experiences of 50 new generation leaders through an interactive process, iterative conceptualization, and within their generational, historical, cultural, and business contexts. ■

Appendix B

RECOMMENDED RESOURCES

LEADERSHIP COACHING AND CONSULTING

For senior-level leaders at both traditional and start-up companies

If you want to unleash the creativity and courage of your teams, customers or partners, and you are inspired to lead with a people-centered approach, or if you're challenged to scale-up your business and want to develop a purpose-driven, agile, people-centered, and collaborative culture, get in touch for an exploratory discussion.

What we could discuss:

- How to deliver the new results you need by designing and implementing a truly effective Change and Transformation Program
- How to design and grow a culture that is agile, values driven and focused on your purpose
- How to help the organization embrace change and innovation by developing leaders and teams with high EQ
- How to improve the effectiveness of inter-departmental collaboration to reduce wasted management time and increase collective impact
- How to help the organization take advantage of the exponential change facing your industry by inspiring Leaders and Managers to envision the future of the business and model leading change for the workforce
- How to create an optimal leadership environment among the senior team by developing a growth-mindset, and by increasing sharing and collaboration
- How to future-proof your business for the inevitable disruption already on its way

Contact Maitri O'Brien at **maitriobrien.com**

HIRE MAITRI O'BRIEN TO SPEAK ON *THE NEW LEADERS OF CHANGE*

Is leading change or next generation leadership a keynote topic for your next leadership event?

The single word that people tend to use when they hear Maitri speak is 'inspirational'. Her message conveys the perfect sense of life wisdom with enlightened playfulness and humour. Your audience is guaranteed cutting-edge research and a high-impact presentation with lessons that will last a lifetime.

To explore how *The New Leaders of Change* could run as a keynote or workshop event contact Maitri O'Brien at **maitriobrien.com**.

BULK COPIES OF *THE NEW LEADERS OF CHANGE*

To order multiple copies of *The New Leaders of Change* for a workshop or event you're running, or simply to share them with your team, contact Maitri O'Brien at **maitriobrien.com**

Appendix C

BIBLIOGRAPHY

Benioff, Mark (2009) *Behind the Cloud: The Untold Story of How Salesforce.com Went from Idea to Billion-Dollar Company-and Revolutionized an Industry* Wiley-Blackwell

Block, Peter (1993) *Stewardship: Choosing Service Over Self-interest* Berrett-Koehler Publishers

Clifton, Donald and Buckingham, Marcus (2004) *Now Discover Your Strengths* Simon and Schuster

Diamandis, Peter and Kotler, Steven (2012) *Abundance: the Future is Better than You Think* Free Press

Dweck, Carol (2006) *Mindset: The New Psychology of Success* Random House

Edmondson, Amy (2018) *The Fearless Organization: Creating Psychological Safety in the Workplace for Learning, Innovation and Growth* Harvard Business Publishing

Elkington, John (2020) *Green Swans: The Coming Boom in Regenerative Capitalism* Fast Company Press

Espindola, David and Wright, Michael (2021) *The Exponential Era: Strategies to Stay Ahead of the Curve in an Era of Chaotic Changes and Disruptive Forces* Wiley/IEEE Press

Fayol, Henri (1916) *Administration Industrielle et Générale*; published in English in 1949 as *General and Industrial Administration*

Gardner, Howard (2006) *Multiple Intelligences: New Horizons in Theory and Practice* Basic Books

Glaser, Barney and Strauss, Anselm (1967) *The Discovery of Grounded Theory: Strategies for Qualitative Research* Chicago: Aldine Publishing Company

Goleman, Daniel (1999) *Working with Emotional Intelligence* Bloomsbury

Gothelf, Jeff and Seiden, Josh (2017) *Sense and Respond* Harvard Business Publishing

Kahneman, Daniel (2011) *Thinking Fast and Slow* Penguin

Kotter, John (1995) 'Leading Change: why transformation efforts fail' *Harvard Business Review* March-April 1995

Kotter, John (1996) *Leading Change* Harvard Business Publishing

Lewin, Kurt (1947) 'Frontiers in Group Dynamics: Concept, Method and Reality in Social Science; Social Equilibria and Social Change' *Human Relations* 1: 5–41

Lieberman, Matthew (2013) *Social: Why Our Brains are Wired to Connect* Crown Publishing Group

Moss Kanter, Rosabeth (1992) *The Challenge of Organizational Change* Harvard Business Publishing

Naisbitt, John (1982) *Megatrends* Grand Central Publishing

Quan-Haase, Anabel and Wellman, Barry (2005) 'Local Virtuality in an Organization' in *Communities and Technologies* van den Besselaar, Peter *et al.* (eds) Milan, Italy

Robertson, Brian (2015) *Holacracy: The Revolutionary Management System that Abolishes Hierarchy* Portfolio Penguin

Savitz, Andrew with Weber, Karl (2006) *The Triple Bottom Line: How Today's Best-run Companies Are Achieving Economic, Social and Environmental Success - And How You Can Too* Jossey Bass

Schein, Edgar (2013) *Humble Inquiry: The Gentle Art of Asking Instead of Telling* Berrett-Koehler

Schwab, Klaus (2016) *The Fourth Industrial Revolution* World Economic Forum

Sedley, David (2003) *Plato's Cratylus* Cambridge University Press

Semler, Ricardo (1993) *Maverick! The Success Story Behind the World's Most Unusual Workplace* Warner

Sutton, Robert (2010) *The No Asshole Rule: Building a Civilised Workplace and Surviving One That Isn't* Piatkus

Taylor, Frederick Winslow (1911) *The Principles of Scientific Management* Harper & Brothers

Worline, M and Dutton, JE, (2017) *Awakening Compassion at Work: The Quiet Power that Elevates People and Organizations* Berrett-Koehler Publishers

Appendix D

NOTES, REFERENCES AND RESOURCES

Chapter 1: The Myth of Managing Change

1 This Heraclitus quote has become very clichéd in use and a lot of spurious internet quotes don't help. But here it is in Plato: 'Heraclitus, I believe, says that all things pass and nothing stays, and comparing existing things to the flow of a river, he says you could not step twice into the same river.' I've listed David Sedley's 2003 edition of Plato's Cratylus in the bibliography, but you can find this online at Stanford University: plato.stanford.edu/entries/heraclitus/

2 You can read more about impermanence across the web, but there are well crafted explanations in the context of Buddhism here: Robert E Buswell Jr and Donald S Lopez Jr (2013) *The Princeton Dictionary of Buddhism*, Princeton University Press pp 42–43, 47, 581

3 They're not the only consultancy or research institution looking at this, but you can learn more about McKinsey's agile research here: mckinsey.com/business-functions/organization/our-insights/the-five-trademarks-of-agile-organizations

4 This Constellation Research survey from 2000-2014, featured in Harvard Business Review, captures the failure of change across a 15-year time period: hbr.org/sponsored/2017/07/digital-transformation-is-racing-ahead-and-no-industry-is-immune-2

5 Many consultancies regularly survey transformation and change – here's KPMG's Global Transformation Study from 2016 which articulates the data well. Later surveys are available, but this one nails the trend. assets.kpmg/content/dam/kpmg/pdf/2016/05/global-transformation-study-2016.pdf

6 The Exponential Era is such a great phrase – check out the bibliography and get hold of *Abundance* by Diamandis and Kotler for their 2012 take on it; more recently (2020) Espindola and Wright have written a whole book on this for Wiley.

7 Hyperconnectivity as a concept first saw the light of day at the turn of the 21st century in the work of Anabel Quan-Haase and Barry Wellman at the University of Toronto in Canada (see bibliography), but it's only becoming a reality now. The crucial organizational shift making it more than just a theoretical concept is a question: how do we, in practical reality, build a hyperconnected, widely collaborative, and agile organization to benefit from digitization and hyperconnective technologies? Perhaps the most useful viable model that's so far emerged is the idea of the open ecosystem, where a vibrant community of traditional companies, start-ups, research institutions, and individuals work with open standards to share, collaborate, and distribute value to customers, employees, and societies. Making this transformation will require letting go of the command-and-control style of managing businesses

and instead managing with purpose, trust, collaboration, experimentation, and some uncertainty about outcomes. But the commercial returns could be worth it. In a 2020 report, McKinsey estimates such ecosystems could add up to $60 trillion to the global economy by 2025. mckinsey.com/business-functions/mckinsey-digital/our-insights/ecosystem-2-point-0-climbing-to-the-next-level

8 According to a range of surveys reported by *Forbes* writers and on Medium sites over the last decade, many Millennials say they are motivated to be leaders because they want to empower others, while far fewer are concerned about salary or the bottom line of the organization they serve. If you're looking for up-to-date data, it's worth checking the major consultancies such as Deloitte, PWC, McKinsey and KPMG which regularly survey next-generation leaders.

Chapter 2: Learning to Lead Exponential Change

9 The Alphabet founders' letters from Larry Page and Sergei Brin are always worth reviewing, but the first one from 2015 is classic: https://abc.xyz/investor/founders-letters/2015/

10 Huawei maintains what researchers call a superfluid structure. Read more around the web, but there's a good case study here in the Ivey Business Journal: iveybusinessjournal.com/learning-from-huaweis-superfluidity/

11 This model of working echoes the thinking of Jeff Gothelf, who started life in America Online (AOL) in the early internet days, designing products and systems. The tools and practices first employed by sense-and-respond software teams were valuable for any team doing anything, he says. (Check out *Sense and Respond* listed in the bibliography.) First, structure your workforce around small, autonomous teams. Then enable those teams and the individuals within them to access feedback on their work directly from the market. Finally, support real-time responses to that feedback, where the teams can independently trial changes prompted by the market to receive further feedback and ultimately improve the product. Develop, test, reiterate. This sounds very much like what is happening at Cloudflare. Also see Jeff's website for more: jeffgothelf.com

12 It shouldn't come as a surprise to anyone that transparency matters. Research papers and articles have been all over the web for at least the last five years on this. Here's just one of them – a report in *Forbes* on an Innovation workshop hosted by Coresight Research: forbes.com/sites/deborahweinswig/2018/05/25/transparency-is-the-new-normal-top-takeaways-from-the-2018-innovation-series

13 Buffer's not the first and it isn't the only firm to release salaries to the public, but it certainly makes a bold statement. buffer.com/transparency. Check out the story of Semco in Ricardo Semler's 1993 book *Maverick* if you're interested in a path-breaking story around this (see bibliography).

14 3M's 15 per cent strategy has lasted 70 years so far. Learn more in this Wall Street Journal review: https://wsj.com/articles/corporate-americas-most-underrated-innovation-strategy-3ms15-rule-11589556171

Chapter 3: Diversity and Inclusion

15 Most consultancies are looking in depth at diversity today, from HR practice Mercer to the main business consultancies. Accenture's *Getting to Equal 2019* report is just one that repays careful reading: https://accenture.com/gb-en/about/inclusion-diversity/_acnmedia/Thought-Leadership-Assets/PDF/Accenture-Equality-Equals-Innovation-Gender-Equality-Research-Report-IWD-2019.pdf

16 I love how Vernā Myers puts this – that diversity doesn't stick without inclusion. Check out more of her thinking right here: https://vernamyers.com/2017/02/04/diversity-doesnt-stick-without-inclusion/

17 Another valuable survey from McKinsey, this time on women in the workplace. Devour this: https://wiw-report.s3.amazonaws.com/Women_in_the_Workplace_2021.pdf

18 Among many others, consultancy group Deloitte has long had something to say on the changing nature of work. This shift, it says in this 2017 report, will inevitably result in 'the reconfiguration of jobs to leverage uniquely human skills: empathy, social and emotional intelligence, the ability to set context and define business problems'. Read the full report here – it catches the mood well: deloitte.com/us/en/insights/deloitte-review/issue-21/navigating-new-forms-of-work.html

19 'Our economic system has only marginal regard for human values and virtues,' say Dierksmeier and Hoegl. 'But the patent disregard for moral norms in business is less an outcome and much more a cause of the present disruptions and system failures.' I don't recommend many academic papers or chapters here, but this is well worth following up. Dierksmeier, Claus and Hoegl, Katherina (2014) 'A Global Ethic for Globalized Business' in *Another State of Mind* Blomme, Robert and van Hoof, Bertine (eds) Palgrave Macmillan

Chapter 4: The New World of Intergenerational Leadership

20 There are as many ways of defining the demographic generations as there are commentators. But here is one worth exploring from the HR Exchange Network, a community of 270,000 HR professionals around the world: hrexchangenetwork.com/employee-engagement/articles/generations-in-the-workplace

21 When it comes to the case for older workers there's a great summary of the key issues here from Josh Bersin and Tomas Chamorro-Premuzic in *Harvard Business Review* online: Bersin, Josh and Chamorro-Premuzic, Tomas (2019) 'The Case for Hiring Older Workers' *Harvard Business Review* 26 September 2019. Online at hbr.org/2019/09/the-case-for-hiring-older-workers

22 As well as my interview with Chip Conley featured in this book, you can find his TEDTalk online, 'What Baby Boomers Can Learn from Millennials at Work', and there are many other books and papers well worth reading. Find them at his website: chipconley.com.

23 For more on the growth mindset explore Carol Dweck's work on mindset through her books – the best is listed in the bibliography – and check out her talk at TEDxNorrkoping in 2014.

24 There is some neuroscience research to suggest we are wired to be social. Matthew Lieberman wrote about this in 2013 in his book *Social*. It's listed in the bibliography.

25 Psychological safety is one of those things we think we know about, but probably not enough to make it work in practical terms. Some striking work on this was published by Amy Edmondson some time ago: Edmondson, Amy (1999) 'Psychological Safety and Learning Behavior in Work Teams' *Administrative Science Quarterly*, 44(2), pp 350-383. But in 2018 she published a mainstream book – *The Fearless Organization* – that's well worth reading. Check it out in the bibliography. If you still need persuading, here's a guide from Google that highlights just how significant psychological safety is for teambuilding. rework.withgoogle.com/print/guides/5721312655835136/ And finally if you want to learn more about putting psychological safety into practice for yourself, you could review the work of Edgar Schein featured in his *Humble Inquiry: The Gentle Art of Asking Instead of Telling*, published in 2013. That's also worth exploring and it's also listed in the bibliography.

Chapter 5: A Call to Adventure

26 Get the full 44-page report here: https://www.americanexpress.com/content/dam/amex/uk/staticassets/pdf/AmexBusinesstheMillennialWay.pdf

27 A good summary of EY's work on purpose and why it matters. Download the PDF here: https://hbr.org/resources/pdfs/comm/ey/19392HBRReportEY.pdf

Chapter 7: Teams are the Heartbeat of the Company

28 See note 25 on how Google builds teams.

29 See note 25 on psychological safety.

30 Get the brilliant *Stewardship* by Peter Block – it's listed in the bibliography. Check out this excerpt here: https://www.bkconnection.com/static/Stewardship_2nd_EXCERPT.pdf

31 The World Economic Forum has long been at the forefront of advocating new ideas for leadership. In this 2016 report it highlights the significance of emotional intelligence which (even at that time) had not been taken seriously enough by employers as a characteristic worth hiring for. weforum.org/docs/WEF_FOJ_Executive_Summary_Jobs.pdf

32 This classic study on the aftermath of rudeness offers a snapshot of what can happen when we allow poor behavior to persist. Porath, Christine and Pearson, Christine (2013) 'The Price of Incivility' in *Harvard Business Review* Jan-Feb 2013 Harvard Business Publishing. When poor behavior becomes toxic the outcomes can be worse, as shown in this Harvard working paper from 2015: hbs.edu/ris/Publication%20Files/16-057_d45c0b4f-fa19-49de-8f1b-4b12fe054fea.pdf

Chapter 8: Transforming the 21st Century Organization

33 There's a swathe of data across the web about the failure of organization-level change programs, a good deal of it from the main consultancies. And there's a salutary lesson I want to share from a 2018 McKinsey report, *Unlocking Success in Digital Transformations*. Fewer than one-third of organizational transformations succeed at improving a company's performance, the report says. And the likelihood of sustaining those gains is even lower. Why? Surprise, surprise, successful digital transformations require cultural and behavioral changes, says McKinsey. So this will remain a challenge for the foreseeable future. Again, why? Well, virtually every company on the *Forbes Global 2000* declares it's on some sort of digital transformation journey. But the vast majority – 84 per cent, according to McKinsey – said they were not prepared to change behavior. If these data hold true for any length of time, this is a disaster in the making facing many of the world's largest corporations.

34 Marc Benioff's V2MOM process has lasted as a process since the tail-end of the 20th century. For that reason alone you should probably learn more about it as a mechanism for sharing values and vision. As a start checkout this LinkedIn post: https://www.linkedin.com/pulse/v2mom-salesforces-company-wide-organizational-annie-nguyen-/

35 As I said in Chapter 1, management as we know it was developed for factories. And it's still very present as a management system today. But every industry today involves complex knowledge work and should involve people at every level of decision-making. So take a look at the work of Holacracy. It's thought-provoking. holacracy.org

36 There have been a range of media reports over the years suggesting that Millennials prefer working for start-ups and that many will actually quit their jobs to do so. You need to be careful interpreting these data, but there does seem to be evidence of a trend.

https://www.forbes.com/sites/larryalton/2017/02/15/are-millennials-more-or-less-likely-to-start-their-own-businesses/?sh=3878c1321301

https://www.npr.org/2016/09/26/495487260/millennials-want-to-be-entrepreneurs-but-a-tough-economy-stands-in-their-way

https://smallbiztrends.com/2017/09/low-number-of-millennial-entrepreneurs.html

37 The well-known Gallup survey is worth a look to remind yourself how engaged, or not, people really are in your business. According to Gallup's 2019 data only 29 per cent of Millennials are engaged at work when the US national average is 34 per cent. Which means many more Millennials feel uninspired, unmotivated and emotionally disconnected from their workplace. But don't get misled by the web's poor reporting on this. Millennials are as likely as anyone else to be loyal to their workplace. What Millennials want is the same thing everybody wants in a job. Millennials just want it more and are less likely to wait around to get it. 'Their refusal to settle for less increases businesses' turnover costs,' says Gallup, 'which bleeds $30.5 billion from the US economy every year.' Take a look at the latest

survey here and then check out Donald Clifton and Marcus Buckingham's *Now Discover Your Strengths* in the bibliography. gallup.com/workplace/267743/why-millennials-job-hopping.aspx

38 The *Financial Times* report on the crisis inside the cult of Travis Kalanick at Uber is instructive. A huge lesson for any entrepreneurial leader. https://www.ft.com/content/9b65a59a-03e1-11e7-ace0-1ce02ef0def9

39 For more on asshole leaders review Bob Sutton's frightening but laugh-out loud book *The No Asshole Rule*. It's from 2010, but is still relevant today. It's all there in the subtitle: building a civilized workplace and surviving one that isn't.

40 There are many surveys available on the web on the take up of digital transformation. According to a solid report by IDC in 2017, three-quarters of enterprises would fail to meet their digital transformation objectives in the decade ahead. It's hard to believe much has changed in the last five years, given what's been happening recently, so that's probably still a reasonably valid yardstick to bear in mind. Search this report online: IDC Futurescape (2017), IDC

Chapter 9: Changing the World

41 Friedman, Milton (1962) *Capitalism and Society* University of Chicago Press. There's a shorter, perhaps an easier read in the New York Times (1970) and you can find it online here: nytimes.com/1970/09/13/archives/a-friedman-doctrine-the-social-responsibility-of-business-is-to.html

42 Read the whole revision here, redefining the purpose of a corporation: https://businessroundtable.org/business-roundtable-redefines-the-purpose-of-a-corporation-to-promote-an-economy-that-serves-all-americans

43 Larry Fink writes regularly to shareholders and all his contacts about long-term strategy, purpose and climate change. Check out the recent letters – they're instructive. https://www.blackrock.com/corporate/investor-relations/larry-fink-ceo-letter

44 In its first 50 years the Davos Manifesto spelled out the vision of the World Economic Forum. Worth comparing the first and the last: https://www.weforum.org/the-davos-manifesto

45 John Elkington's impact has been huge in sustainability consulting, not least for coining the phrase triple bottom line. Learn more here: https://johnelkington.com/archive/TBL-elkington-chapter.pdf and see Green Swans listed in the bibliography.

46 Marking the report's 10th anniversary, the *2021 Millennial and Gen Z Survey* by Deloitte reveals two generations demanding social change and accountability.

47 This is backed up by 2017 research, *Championing Change in the Age of Social Media*, from Sprout Social, the social media consultancy, who suggest that two-thirds of consumers feel it's important for brands to take a public stance on leading social and political issues like immigration, human rights and race relations.

48 On May 5 2020 Patrick Pouyanné, Chairman of the Board at Total, said: 'Energy

markets are changing, driven by climate change, technology and societal expectations. Total is committed to helping solve the dual challenge of providing more energy with fewer emissions. We are determined to advance the energy transition while also growing shareholder value. Today, we are announcing our new Climate Ambition to get to Net Zero by 2050 - together with society. The Board believes that Total's global roadmap, strategy and actions set out a path that is consistent with goals of the Paris agreement. We acknowledge the positive role of engagement and open dialog with investors as the one we experienced with Climate 100+ along the last months.'

https://www.total.com/media/news/total-adopts-new-climate-ambition-get-net-zero-2050

49 Get the story about Skor's stepping down as reported in the Financial Times. https://ft.com/content/f6879271-f5f2-49f7-bdb7-d6edb06de7f5

50 Check out Solomon's opinion piece in the Financial Times here: https://ft.com/content/ffd794c8-183a-11ea-b869-0971bffac109

Chapter 10: Towards People-Centered Leadership

51 The original and the best definitions of social identity and in-groups come from Henri Tajfel. This is his original work here and it's well worth exploring: Tajfel, H, Turner, J C, Austin, WG, & Worchel, S (1979) 'An integrative theory of intergroup conflict' *Organizational Identity: A Reader*, 56-65.

52 Personal identity is a much looser construct than social identity, but Eric Olsen summarizes it well here: Olson, Eric T, 'Personal Identity', *The Stanford Encyclopedia of Philosophy* (Spring 2021 Edition), Edward N Zalta (ed). It's also available online: https://plato.stanford.edu/entries/identity-personal/

53 For a full breakdown of the Wicked 7 problems see this site led by Philip Kotler and Christian Sarkar: https://www.wicked7.org/

54 Here's the Wharton article summarizing Jeff Weiner's speech on compassion. Well worth reading. https://knowledge.wharton.upenn.edu/article/linkedin-ceo-how-compassion-can-build-a-better-company/

55 *Training* magazine continues to share valuable insights on leadership development more than 50 years since its launch. This is a recent survey worth exploring. https://trainingmag.com/annual-leadership-development-survey-the-times-they-are-a-changing/

INDEX

G

H

I

Q

R

S

X

Y

Z

About the Author
MAITRI O'BRIEN

Maitri O'Brien is the Business Transformation Partner at AS Equity Partners. She is responsible for helping the firm's portfolio companies drive growth and business transformation – coupled with coaching and consulting the executive leadership team across the portfolio. She is a key operating partner with particular focus on change, transformation, and leadership development in companies in which AS Equity Partners invests.

Prior to her role at AS Equity Partners, O'Brien held leadership roles in Change and Transformation consulting in Hewlett-Packard, HPE and DXC Technologies, where she sold and delivered business change and transformation programs for *Fortune* 500 companies across North and South America, Continental Europe, UK and Asia.

Throughout her 25+ year career in business transformation consulting, O'Brien has covered a wide range of issues including change and transformation management, organization and operating model design, employee engagement and multi-stakeholder management, leadership development and coaching. She has extensive experience in M&As, complex transformations and restructuring.

She is from San Francisco, California, and currently lives in Zurich, Switzerland. 'I am particularly passionate about putting the people in the center of change and transformation. I believe successful and agile organizations are focused on engaging, energizing and empowering their employees and customers while ensuring leaders are transformative, inclusive and people-centric.'

Connect on LinkedIn
https://www.linkedin.com/in/maitriobrien/

Join the movement
maitriobrien.com

Made in the USA
Monee, IL
12 November 2026

f50ac4f1-73d7-48c9-b386-948135f2fa4dR01